Some Women Amazed Us

Biblical Studies from a Christian
Feminist Perspective

Bernice Santor
2003

Permissions

Appreciation is expressed for permission to use the following material:

Carole Etzler, "Standing Before Us", 1180 VT Route 22A, Bridport, VT 05734, U.S.A.

Miriam Therese Winter, "A Psalm to Widen our Tents", from *WomanWisdom*. New York: Crossroad, 1991.

Rigoberta Menchu Tum, "Your Gaze", from *Through the Eyes of a Woman*. Geneva, World Council of Churches, 1995.

Paul L. Maier, Trans. and Ed. *Josephus: The Essential Writings*. Grand Rapids: Kregel, 1988, p. 177.

Scripture quotations and all biblical references are from the *New Revised Standard Version of the Bible*, copyright ©1989 by the Division of Christian Education of the National Council of the Churches of Christ in the U.S.A. Used by permission. All rights reserved.

Every reasonable effort has been made to find copyright holders. The author would be grateful to have any errors or omissions brought to her attention.

Copies of *Some Women Amazed Us* can be ordered from:

Bernice Santor
Box 924
10321 Dogwood Crescent
Grand Bend, Ontario N0M 1T0
santor@hay.net
519-238-1078

ISBN 0-9733029-0-9

Printed in Canada by: The Aylmer Express Ltd.
Fine Print Division
Production: Michelle Barrett
Layout & Design: Denise Ward

For Ekklesia,

A Christian Feminist Group in London, Canada

Acknowledgments

I want to express a special thanks to my husband Don who has been my guide and editor throughout this whole project. He has helped me to clarify my ideas and present them in a direct and meaningful way. I also want to acknowledge his assistance in promoting and marketing the book.

A debt of gratitude is owed to Gefen Bar-On, a doctoral candidate, Department of English, McGill University, who read the original manuscript and made valuable suggestions for sentence structure and language that resulted in a much more "polished" book than I would have written without her assistance, and to Sandra Cox for proof reading the final manuscript.

I want to express my appreciation to Garth Santor and Trinh Han who took my line drawings and transformed them into computer graphics and for their work in photographing the quilts. I also want to thank my family and friends who have encouraged me to write this book and have shown such enthusiasm for the whole project.

In addition, a special thank you is owed to the Women's Inter-Church Council of Canada for their financial support and enthusiastic encouragement. All profits from the sale of the books will be donated for the work of the Women's Inter-Church Council in celebration of its 85th anniversary.

The quilts, monologues and line drawings are the creation of the author. For any errors or omissions in the manuscript, I take full responsibility.

Contents

Introduction

> *The time has come to share with the people in the parish the fruit of the last quarter century of work. Not all questions have been answered, not all problems solved, but enough progress has been made that a vast amount of refreshing, exciting—sometimes disturbing—material needs to be shared broadly, freely discussed, and evaluated by those whose lives are touched by these issues in very practical ways.*
>
> *Alice Ogden Bellis, Helpmates, Harlots, and Heroes, 1994.*

For the past six years I have been speaking to both religious and secular groups about the women of the Bible. In my presentations I used five quilted wall hangings to tell the stories of Eve, Huldah, Mary Magdalene, the Woman at the Well and Martha, with the intention to raise awareness for the possibility of discovering alternative, non-traditional interpretations. I have been quite overwhelmed by the encouraging and enthusiastic responses to these presentations. Many women spoke about their own experiences with the traditional interpretations of these stories. They expressed concern and even anger that the biblical women had so often been used as examples of the "forgiven sinner" whose lives were used as models for all women. They were upset to learn that the contributions of biblical women to the growth and success of their religious communities have been ignored by the religious leadership and set aside as unimportant and insignificant. At the same time many felt empowered when they discovered that there was more than one way to interpret and proclaim these stories. Men who heard the presentation responded either with encouraging enthusiasm or indifference.

Because of these responses to my presentation, I came to the conclusion that women wanted and needed to rediscover biblical women who would inspire and encourage them in their faith and ministry. As Bellis suggests in the quotation above, it is time to take a fresh look at scripture by setting aside old interpretations and searching for a new response to the biblical women's stories.

In this study I am not trying to rescue the Bible as an apologist, arguing that everything contained there is valuable and beyond criticism. There is no need to do that. The Bible has its own integrity if it is studied, not as a book of rules and regulations, but as a source of inspiration and insight that can lead to dialogue and discussion. We must be able to critique what we read in scripture, realizing that not everything presented there will be helpful for our situation today. At the same time, we must value the record of the Hebrew people's struggle to understand who they were, why they came into existence, and how they understood the divine presence in their lives. Scripture records women's stories as being an integral part of the Hebrew journey of understanding.

From the many women named in scripture, I have chosen twelve as examples of those who have been misunderstood, ignored or diminished by biased and unfair interpretations. I use a feminist theological methodology to search for new meanings. One of the most important requirements of this methodology is for women to ask critical questions that come from a woman's curiosity about the text. As well, women are encouraged to connect their life experiences with the text. It is also important to draw upon recent archeological discoveries as well as ancient texts that go beyond the biblical record. Both of these areas of scholarship will provide valuable information for understanding what lies behind the text in its historical setting.

This exegetical study deals seriously with the need to understand the original setting and intention of the text in order to reclaim it for use in today's society. After this exegesis has been done, each member of the study group is encouraged to express a response to the text in creative and meaningful ways.

Using This Book

1. This study book is designed for small group participation, but it can be adapted for other situations. An individual can learn a great deal by working through all the questions and biblical references, but may miss the insights that can come from sharing ideas in a group situation. The material in this book provides information that can also be helpful in sermon preparation. It provides insights that can raise the awareness and acceptance of these women's stories as a source of inspiration and challenge for Christians today.
2. There is a role for a facilitator, but it does not always need to be the same person. The facilitator's task is to guide and direct the discussion based on the information and questions provided in the study. Most impor-

tantly, the facilitator must ensure that every member has an equal opportunity to share in the discussion.

3. Each study has more than enough material for one session. Participants should spend as much time as needed to fully understand the selected texts. Since biblical writers have woven a number of complex ideas into the narratives, serious and continued study is necessary to reveal all that the text contains and to open it to greater insight and learning. If enough time and study are devoted to the texts, these women's stories will become treasures that will inspire, challenge and empower those who come to know them intimately.
4. While many editions of the Bible can be used for this study, it is necessary to have access to the Apocrypha. This study guide is based on the *New Revised Standard Version of the Bible*, Division of Christian Education of the National Council of the Churches of Christ, U.S.A., 1989.
5. Every session begins with a brief introduction that highlights the important contribution of each woman. It provides an overview of the woman's role within her faith community and challenges the traditional interpretation of her story.
6. At the beginning of each session participants should read the text aloud as well as silently. Many of these texts originate from an oral tradition and were to be read aloud to a receptive audience. Try to listen to the text as if you are hearing it for the first time. After the text has been read, it is important for the participants to express their initial response along with any new insights or questions that may arise. Keep the questions before the group as it works through the session. Do not be afraid to ask any question no matter how insignificant it may appear to be. It may be the one that opens up a new understanding of the story.
7. This study focuses on three areas of exegesis—literary form, word study and historical context (known as *Sitz im Leben*)—as a way to understand the original intention and meaning of the text. A discussion of the literary form of the text will provide insight as to whether the text is to be understood as history, narrative, poetry or some other form of writing. The word study is designed to uncover the ancient concepts that are embedded in particular words and how these words are effectively used to convey deeper insights into the meaning of the text. A study of the historical context provides the background for understanding the original purpose and intention of the writer. It helps to answer the questions of where, why and for whom it was written. Participants are encouraged to examine all the biblical references provided. Much can be learned by cross-referencing texts within scripture itself.

8. In each session questions are provided as a way to become familiar with the text and to assist in its interpretation and meaning. The study group may raise other questions for consideration as well. The questions may not be easily answered, but the discussion and dialogue by group members can lead to exciting new ways to interpret these stories.
9. The stories of biblical women deal with social, religious and political situations in their time and place. These stories can be reclaimed to provide insight into the social, religious and political issues we encounter today. They can provide the foundation for discussing our present day concerns about racism, religious intolerance, poverty and sexism, to name but a few.
10. The "Creative Imagination" section encourages participants to give creative expression to new insights learned from the biblical text. Understanding the depth of meaning found in the text can be expressed in artistic and creative ways using many different mediums such as paper, paint, fabric or clay. I have discovered from leading workshops that there is a wealth of talent among the participants who need only to be challenged and nurtured to express themselves. The Jewish practice of *midrash* (a literary technique that retells the story by filling in the silences in the text) is an exciting and creative way to express a new understanding of the story. Two excellent examples of midrash can be found in Anita Diamant's *The Red Tent* and Miriam Therese Winter's *The Chronicles of Noah and Her Sisters* (see Bibliography).
11. The closing ritual of each session is designed to give communal expression to the most salient teachings of each text. Sitting in a circle where everyone can see each other helps to facilitate the sharing of ideas and reflections arising from the study. Participants are encouraged to make additions to the ritual that reflect the spiritual insights and practices of their own communities.
12. The bibliography lists some of the books and music that have been my source of knowledge and inspiration for writing this book. Participants will be greatly rewarded if they choose any or all of them for further study.

The Bible is a collection of stories and accounts rich with insight into the human-divine condition. It deserves to be studied seriously using all the tools available. It is my hope that this book will provide the necessary challenge to take the participants on a spiritual journey that will be both rewarding and insightful.

Eve: The Mother of All Living

The man named his wife Eve, because she was the mother of all living.
Genesis 3:20

Scripture Texts: *Genesis 1:1-2:4a;*
Genesis 2:4b-3:24.

Introduction

For generations Eve has been the symbol of "woman" as a sexual seductress who brought sin and evil into a once perfect world. This description of Eve's character came not so much from scripture itself, but from traditions and folklore that were imposed on the biblical text.

The early church developed a theology from the story of Adam and Eve which came to be known as "Fall-Redemption Theology." This understanding of God's relationship to humanity professes that all humans are fallen creatures who need to be saved from sin. It declares that the man, Adam, and especially the woman, Eve, were responsible for humanity's separation from God.

It is the purpose of this study to question the negative portrayal of Eve and to consider an alternative understanding of humanity's relationship to God. The study will involve a close examination of the relevant texts, allowing each to tell its own story. By reclaiming a new image of Eve, we may discover an image of God that has been ignored by church teachings.

Step I: Getting Acquainted with the Text

1. Read the text silently and then ask a participant to read it aloud.
2. Give your immediate response to the passages. What are your feelings regarding the text?
3. Jot down any questions you have about the text. Look for the answers as you complete the study.

Step II: Understanding the Text

1. Literary Form

The history of Israel was written in the form of an epic composed of episodes that related the achievements of ancient heroes, leaders and kings. The writers of this epic borrowed many legendary tales from other countries such as Assyria, Greece and Babylon. The story of Noah's ark from Genesis chapters 7 and 8 can also be found in the Babylonian *Epic of Gilgamesh* that was recorded in the early centuries of the second millennium BCE. The ancient Hebrews adapted these traditional stories to their own particular understanding of God and of humanity's relationship to the divine.

The Hebrew epic about Israel's history begins with two creation stories that set the stage for further episodes about Noah, Abraham, Sarah, Jacob, Joseph, Moses, Miriam and Aaron. These two creation stories should be studied in the context of the epic as a whole.

The oldest creation story written by the Yahwist author (named the J account by scholars) is found in Genesis, chapters 2 and 3 and takes the form of a narrative. The Priestly (or P account) is found in Genesis 1 and provides an orderly account of creation. Because of the differences in style and language, scholars can easily determine that Genesis contains two distinct creation accounts. These two accounts are known as "aetiological" stories because they try to explain why things are the way they are. Such stories should be understood as descriptive of past or present events, rather than prescriptive of future behaviour or action.

Compare the two creation stories in Genesis:

- How are they similar in their attempt to explain the creation of humankind? How are they different?
- How do they describe humanity's relationship to God?
- How is Eve portrayed in each account?

2. Word Study

It is unfortunate that English translations do not always convey the subtleties of the original Hebrew language. As a result, the full meaning of the text is not readily understood by the reader. The oldest creation story contains several examples where Hebrew words are used as puns that provide an additional dimension to the story.

human and ground: (Genesis 2:7)
Adam is the Hebrew word for a human being. When this word is first used in the text it designates no particular gender. Later in the story the same word is used as a name for the husband of Eve. *Adamah* is the Hebrew word for the ground or earth. The *adam* was made from the *adamah*. The words *adam and adamah* are formed from the same word root. The use of these two closely related words emphasizes the relationship between humanity and the earth.

man and woman: (Genesis 2:23)
When God creates Eve to be an appropriate companion for Adam, two gender-specific humans came into being. The narrator of the story introduces two new words to describe them, *ish* and *ishshah*. The word *ish* in Hebrew is a gender-specific name for a man or a husband. *Ishshah* is the gender specific name for a woman or wife.

Phyllis Trible points out in *God and the Rhetoric of Sexuality* that *ish* and *ishshah* are used to describe the man and the woman only during the part of the story where they are living in harmony. When the harmony is broken by disobedience, the narrator again uses Adam to name the man, and the woman is given a new name, Eve.

Although the words *ish* and *ishshah* sound much the same, they are derived from different roots. The narrator may be using these words as a pun to emphasize that the man and the woman who are separate beings also depend on each other.

helper: (Genesis 2:20)
This word in Hebrew (*ezer*) conveys the idea of a companion who is an appropriate partner. It does not imply inferiority as English usage may suggest. This same word is used to describe God on several occasions (Exodus 18:4; Deuteronomy 33:7; Psalm 33:20 and 124:8).

3. Historical Context

The annihilation of the Northern Kingdom of Israel by the Assyrians in 722 BCE had a devastating effect on the Southern Kingdom of Judah. The Judeans lived with the fear that they could suffer the same fate. Judah was a small nation constantly struggling to survive in the midst of such great nations as Egypt, Assyria and Babylon. Because of the constant threat to their identity, the Hebrew people needed a written history that would give meaning to their existence and empower them to live as God's people. Their history begins with the creation story of Adam and Eve and then proceeds to show how God continues to be involved in the activities of humankind.

Step III: Interpreting the Text

Two of the key players in the narrative story of creation are Eve and God. Answer the following questions to determine their specific roles:

Part A: Eve's Role (Genesis 2 and 3)

The Creation of Eve

- Why did God decide to create Eve?
- How was she different from the animals? Why was that difference important?
- Is there evidence in the story to show that Eve was inferior to Adam?

Harmony Disrupted

- Who was given the initial instruction by God not to eat the fruit? When did God give this warning?
- The Bible does not explicitly state that the fruit was an apple. Why do you think interpreters later named it an apple?
- Why did Eve decide to eat the fruit?
- Did Eve trick or seduce Adam? Was Eve's sin the "tempting of Adam" as so many theologians have suggested?
- What was Eve's sinful act? What was Adam's?
- Did Adam and Eve's sinful act have anything to do with sexuality?
- Both Adam and Eve disobeyed God's command. In what way was their act of disobedience different?

Consequence

- What human condition was revealed to Adam and Eve when they ate the fruit?
- How was each of them "punished"?
- Was Eve's "punishment" greater than Adam's? Was the "punishment" meant to be for all future men and women? How did the "punishments" reflect the social situations of men and women at the time when the story

was written?

- Before they left the garden, what name did Adam give to his wife? Speculate why he gave her this title.

Conclusion

- Describe the character of Eve as it can be determined from the story in Genesis. What are her strengths and her weaknesses?
- Does the biblical story support the traditional interpretation of Eve as a sexual sinner, an undisciplined female, an inferior creation or the cause of evil in the world? What evidence refutes such an interpretation and points instead to a different understanding of Eve?

Part B: God's Role (Genesis 2 and 3)

- Does the account of creation in Genesis 2 and 3 convey the idea that it was God's intention that Adam should dominate the woman Eve? What evidence supports your answer? (Compare to the P account in Genesis 1:26-31.)
- Was the threat that God made to Adam regarding the forbidden fruit actually realized?
- Did the serpent deceive Eve when it claimed that God would not kill her and Adam?
- Despite their disobedience to God's command, what action by God shows that God did not abandon them?
- What reason does God give for Adam and Eve's expulsion from the garden? Speculate why God would make such a response.
- God is the central figure in the epic history of Israel of which the creation story is only one part. How is God portrayed throughout the epic?
- By referring to examples from later Hebrew scripture and the gospel writings, what evidence is there that God continues to interact with humanity and creation?

Step IV: Reclaiming the Scriptures for Today

- If Eve is not clearly defined in scripture as an evil, sexual seductress, where do you think these ideas came from?
- Name some of the ways such an interpretation of Eve has affected the lives of women today and throughout history. In particular, how has it contributed to violence against women around the world?
- What must the church do to change the perception of Eve as a sexual sin-

ner? How can she be portrayed in a more favourable light? Can she be held up as a "model" or inspiration for humankind as it struggles to understand itself?

- Early Church Fathers such as Augustine (354-430) interpreted the story of Adam and Eve as humanity's original sin. More recently Matthew Fox and others have suggested that the creation story describes an original blessing that needs to be celebrated. How has the concentration on Eve as an especially "terrible" sinner detracted from the idea that creation was a blessing to be enjoyed, celebrated and cared for?
- What is your image of God after having completed this study? What kind of theology would you create based on what you have discovered from these creation stories?
- What other insights have you gained from studying these scripture passages?

Creative Imagination

- Fill in the silences of the Genesis story by creating a conversation between Adam and Eve just before they eat the fruit or when they decide to hide from God.
- Write a poem about the "mother of all living" highlighting her contribution to the human story.
- Write a children's story about Adam and Eve from a feminist theological perspective.
- Suggest ways that the "apple" can be a positive symbol of inspiration for women. Make a banner celebrating the "apple".
- Other ideas....

Closing Ritual: Celebrating Creation

Create a ritual focus in the center of a circle by arranging a collection of objects from nature such as leaves, stones, flowers, weeds, shells, twigs, etc.

Play quiet nature music or sounds.

Ask the participants to choose an object from the ritual center that symbolizes an experience where they have felt to be one with nature and close to the sacred. Then give the participants an opportunity to share this experience with the group as they return their objects to the ritual center.

Celebrate creation by sharing a basket or platter of fruit and eating the fruit as a communion activity.

Close the ritual by saying together:

We give thanks
for the richness of creation,
for the challenges it sets before us,
for the life it promises.
Amen

Ruth

She is the Moabite who came back with Naomi from the country of Moab.
Ruth 2:6b

Scripture Texts: *Ruth 1-4.*

Introduction

The book of Ruth is a beautifully written story expressing a complex range of ideas about compassion, acceptance and survival. This is one of several biblical stories about women "who built up the house of Israel" (Ruth 4:11). Ruth takes her place beside Esther, Abigail, Tamar, Rachel and Leah as women who are celebrated as Israel's heroes.

While it is a story about love, friendship and devotion, it is also about the important role that self-determined women played in Israelite society. Looking more deeply into this dramatic story, the reader discovers yet another theme—the concept of redemption. The story describes how bitterness and despair can change to hope and renewal and demonstrates what it means to live in a covenantal relationship with God.

The story revolves around the willingness of Ruth to assume the role of God's agent, as one who works for justice among the people. Ruth shows great strength of character when she decides to leave her homeland and risk an unknown future with her mother-in-law, Naomi. Ruth is willing to accept the guidance of Naomi in order to secure their survival. Her story endures as a source of inspiration for those who feel rejection or despair.

Step I: Getting Acquainted with the Text

1. The entire text of Ruth should be read as one would read a short story. Ask each participant to read it in preparation for the session and to jot down any questions that may arise.

2. If time permits, read the story aloud when the group meets.
3. Ask each participant to share an initial response to the story before continuing with the study.

Step II: Understanding the Text

1. Literary Form

Most biblical scholars classify the book of Ruth as a novella rather than an historical account. Although the story is set in an historical context, its main purpose is not to inform the readers about an event in history, but rather to teach them how to live in a covenantal relationship with God.

It is a spiritual story that uses literary devices such as metaphors, contrasts and visions to inspire its readers to adopt a way of life that will lead to reward and happiness. Because of its many layers of meaning and its use of diverse literary devices, this book is considered to be an extraordinary literary achievement.

Look for examples in the text of:

- Metaphors: No longer call me Naomi which means pleasantness, call me Mara which means bitter (Ruth 1:20-21).
- Contrasts: Orpah and Ruth (Ruth 1).
- Visions: From despair (Ruth 1:3-5) to hope (Ruth 4:13-15).

2. Word Study

hesed:

Hesed is the Hebrew word meaning "loving kindness" which exemplifies the essence of Jewish teaching from the Torah and provides a biblical vision for humanity's relationship to God. In the story of Ruth, kindness to one's own kin is transformed into a greater understanding of *hesed*—the kindness that should be shown to an alien or stranger. *Hesed* is understood to be both a private and a public response to another person's need.

There are several examples in the Bible where the idea of *hesed* goes beyond the obligation of generosity to one's own people (Luke 10:30-37 and Matthew 15:21-28). While *hesed* is an attribute of God (Exodus 34:6), people can express it as well. When they do, they become agents of God, reflecting and fulfilling God's divine purposes (Ruth 1:16 and 4:11-12).

Moabites:
The Moabites were an ancient tribe of people who occupied the land east of the Dead Sea and south of the Arnon River. They settled the area long before the Israelites came in search of the Promised Land. The Israelites looked upon the Moabites as a sexually perverse race of people. According to Hebrew scripture, the Moabites were the result of an incestuous relationship (Genesis 19:30-38). They were perceived to be a licentious, deceptive people (Numbers 25:1-3). When the Israelites were passing through the territory of Moab en route to the Promised Land, the Moabites treated them with hostility. From that time on the Israelites excluded them from their community and were commanded by scripture to treat them with disdain (Deuteronomy 23:3-6). The long history of animosity between the two tribes is even recorded by the prophets of the post-exilic period who warned against association with the Moabites (Ezra 9:1-2; 10:2-3; Nehemiah 13:1-3). The author reminds the reader many times that Ruth came from this despised and hated tribe (Ruth 1:22; 2:2; 2:6,21; 4:5,10).

- Why do you think the author stressed that Ruth was an alien?

levirate marriage:
Levirate law in ancient Israel required a man to marry his dead brother's wife if she had no son to inherit the land. Because this law was intended to preserve the dead man's family name as well as his property, the first son born would keep his deceased father's name. If the brother of the deceased refused to accept this obligation, the widow could shame him by declaring publicly that he had refused. As a sign of his refusal, his sandal could be removed and the widow could spit in his face. Most widows could not be financially independent, so this law assured their security and protection. The story of Tamar (Genesis 38) provides a vivid example of a woman who was exercising her widow's rights.

- How was this levirate right used by Naomi and Ruth (Ruth 4)?

3. Historical Context

Some biblical scholars believe that Ruth was written in pre-exilic times during the period of the judges (Ruth 1:1). At that time the Israelites were still a tribal people and not yet a nation. Because their national boundaries were not rigidly determined, intermarriage may not have been a major concern, and consequently aliens may have been more accepted than they were in later years.

Other biblical scholars suggest there are indications within the story that it may have been written at a much later date—after the return of the Israelites from Babylon. By this time Israel was a nation needing to protect itself against outside influences that may have weakened them as a people. On the return from Babylon the prophets Ezra (9:1-4) and Nehemiah (13:1-3 and 23-25) urged the Israelites to get rid of their foreign wives and children because they were a threat to the purity of their religion. The book of Ruth, on the other hand, accepts foreign wives.

- Reflect on the following hypothesis: Ruth was written as a reaction to the expulsion of foreigners and it was a subversive attempt on the part of a more liberal faction in Israel to react against exclusiveness.
- How does the story of Ruth challenge these reactionary ideas?
- Does the author feel that the acceptance of foreigners would enrich the Hebrew society?

Step III: Interpreting the Text

Demanding Justice

- What evidence can be found in this story to indicate that Ruth and Naomi lived in a patriarchal society?
- Both men and women supported many of the same goals for the Israelite nation. Which of these goals had a special importance for women?
- Which of Ruth and Naomi's actions made it possible for them to overcome some of the patriarchal restrictions on their lives?
- What qualities did Ruth and Naomi possess that enabled them to accomplish their goals?
- Why might Israelites uphold Ruth as a saviour figure?

Accepting the Alien

- Ruth was acting as a substitute for Naomi even though she was a Moabite. How was Ruth received by the women of Bethlehem (Ruth 4:13–17) and by Boaz (2:4–13)? Explain why they responded to her in this way.
- What risks did Ruth take to secure a future for herself and Naomi? Why was it necessary for Ruth to do this? What rules had to be changed for justice to prevail?

Hesed as Divine and Human

- Describe the events that move this story from darkness and despair to hope and new beginnings.

- Describe the different kinds of *hesed* found in the book of Ruth.
- How does this story reflect and affirm the image of God as portrayed in other books of the Bible such as in Exodus 34:6 or Isaiah 56:6-8?
- The book of Ruth is read during the Jewish festival of Shavuot because it represents the heart of the biblical vision of a covenantal community. It is a time to renew the covenant between God and the people. How would this story challenge the community both then and now to live up to its ideals?

Step IV: Reclaiming the Scripture for Today

- In what ways are Ruth and Naomi good role models for women today?
- How is the concept of God enlarged by this story? Compare the story of Ruth with the story of "The Good Samaritan" (Luke 10:30–37) or the "Woman at the Well" (John 4:7–24). How is God portrayed in these New Testament stories? How are they similar to the message in Ruth?
- How can this story foster understanding and compassion toward immigrants and refugees coming to your country?
- What are some of the complaints that people in our society make against immigrants and refugees? In what ways do we marginalize ethnic and minority groups in our society?
- Ruth's commitment to Naomi brought new life and opportunities not only for themselves but also for the entire community. How do immigrants and refugees enrich our society?

Creative Imagination

- Research the *Shavuot* Festival or invite a Jewish woman to tell your group about this event in her community. Share some of the foods and activities from this celebration.
- Write a poem about the experience of *hesed* in your life.
- Write a prayer celebrating the universal God who loves and cares for all people.
- Create a poster or a wall hanging using symbols and slogans welcoming immigrants and refugees to our country.
- Other ideas....

Closing Ritual: Sharing our Lives with Strangers

Meditation Center: Create a display of symbols to represent hospitality such as a cup of water or coffee, oil for the head and feet, and a loaf of bread.

Invite participants to share stories about encounters with people from another country, either in their own community or while visiting other parts of the world.

Play Carolyn McDade's *Song of Community* (see Bibliography) to provide some time for meditative thought before sharing the stories.

Invite participants to share their stories.

Complete the storytelling by passing bread as a symbol of our willingness to share our lives with strangers.

Close the ritual by reading together:

Your Gaze, by Rigoberta Menchu Tum.

Your full, sincere, tranquil, tender gaze,
like the stars, the fresh breeze and
the songs of sunrise dawning.

She is the one who crossed borders and did not have
time to say farewell to her betrothed, disappeared,
she who cried out truth to the world,
gave a speech before military assassins,
and whose voice did not break.
She is the one who conquered her fear,
accepted solitude as her companion in distant lands,
crossed borders wailing for a plane from here to there and back again.

She is the daughter, the granddaughter of the Maya,
She is the one who was born under a blue sky.
She is the memory of Chimel.
It is for you, beautiful woman of my land.
(Used with permission)

Abigail

As she rode on the donkey and came down under cover of the mountain,
David and his men came down toward her; and she met them.

I Samuel 25:20

Scripture Texts: *I Samuel 25:2-42.*

Introduction

Abigail lived in a patriarchal society where inheritance was passed from father to son. As owners of the land, men could acquire significant wealth and power, but women were given a lower status, always considered to be under the supervision of a father, brother or husband. The norms of society required that men were to provide for and protect the community (the public sphere), while women were to give birth to children and create stability for the well-being of the family unit (the private sphere). This division of roles became more and more institutionalized as the tribes of Israel evolved into a centralized and powerful nation.

Strong, determined women sometimes broke the barriers caused by the development of these stereotypical roles. In fact, biblical women are often portrayed as agents of God who are able to save Israel from moral degeneration or complete annihilation. The literature of Israel has preserved many of these women's stories, for example: Esther, Judith, Susannah, Ruth and Abigail. Perhaps they were written to remind us that women did participate in bringing forth God's justice, despite the norms of society that suggested that such activities were reserved for men. The virtues of wisdom, compassion, reconciliation and courage evident in these women challenged the hierarchical institutions that oppressed them. The literature of Israel is testimony to the contribution that women made to the growth and development of both the religious and political life of Israel.

Step I: Getting Acquainted with the Text

1. Read the text silently and then choose a participant to read it aloud.
2. What are your feelings regarding the text? Share your general impressions or immediate response to the passages.
3. Jot down any questions you have about the text. Look for the answers as you complete the study.

Step II: Understanding the Text

1. Literary Form

The two books of Samuel contain the stories of three of Israel's great leaders: Samuel, Saul and David. These books are part of the Deuteronomistic History that records the growth and development of Israel. These accounts are a mixture of historical narratives, commentary and storytelling. Very little can be verified by referring to sources outside scripture, so readers are cautioned not to look upon all passages as accurate historical information.

- Do you think that Abigail's story is historical fact or storytelling? Give reasons for your opinion. Even if the account is only storytelling, what can we learn from it about the history of Israel and the role of women?

2. Word Study

Nabal: (I Samuel 25:3, 25, 36-38)
Hebrew scripture frequently gives characters in stories names that describe who they are or how they will act. Abigail's husband Nabal has such a name. As a verb the Hebrew word *nabal* means to be foolish or senseless; as an adjective it often refers to someone who is irreligious and has no respect for ethical behaviour. This person is considered to be churlish and arrogant, and will very likely suffer a humiliating death. Nabal's strange death would not be a surprise to the audience who heard his story because his name foreshadowed his end.

- What words are used to describe Nabal?

Calebite: (I Samuel 25:2-3)
Nabal and Abigail were Calebites, a tribe of people foreign to Israel. Nabal held property in Carmel and sheared his sheep there.

- How would David's marriage to Abigail, who was the widow of a wealthy Calebite chieftain, be of benefit to David as he tried to secure the throne of Israel?

bloodguilt: (I Samuel 25:26-31)
The word *bloodguilt* refers to the shedding of blood without just cause. At the time of the encounter of David and Nabal, David was not yet King of Israel. Saul became very jealous when Samuel gave his blessing to David (I Samuel 16:1-13). Because Saul wanted to kill David, David was forced to flee (I Samuel 21:10). He began to build his own power base in the desert area of Judah. As the leader of a band of mercenaries who protected the southern tribes from desert raiders, David was able to win their loyalty. When David was about to annihilate Nabal's household, Abigail reminded David that God favoured him because he had been fighting God's battles (I Samuel 23:1-5). It would not be acceptable for a future king to have shed the blood of innocent people out of senseless anger.

3. Historical Context

Can Abigail's behaviour be considered typical of women's roles in ancient Israel? This is an important question. In Israel and the surrounding nations women were not permitted to participate in any decision-making that affected the public sphere. In general, they had little authority or influence beyond their own household; however, this situation was sometimes different for women belonging to royalty or wealthy families. Because these women were given the authority to oversee and manage their households, which may include servants and slaves as well as family members, they acquired a certain amount of power and recognition. Such a woman is portrayed in Proverbs 31:10–31.

- Was Abigail assuming her proper role by protecting her household against David's anger, or was she a clever woman who, in the light of Nabal's foolishness, took the necessary steps to secure a future for herself? Give reasons for your opinion.

Step III: Interpreting the Text

- What caused the crisis between David and Nabal? Was David's request reasonable? How serious was Nabal's refusal to respond to that request?
- From Abigail's quick response to David's threat we are able to get a

glimpse of her character. What do we learn about the kind of woman she was? David was prepared to go to war to solve his problems. What "weapons" did Abigail use to overcome the crisis?

- Should Abigail be considered "a prophet and saviour" of Israel (I Samuel 25:32-35)?
- What impresses you most about Abigail? Do you approve or disapprove of the way she placated David? Give reasons.

Step IV: Reclaiming the Scriptures for Today

- Can Abigail be a model of inspiration for women today? Discuss why or why not.
- Abigail was able to prevent a war through acts of reconciliation. How does her story provide insight into the reconciliation process?
- Throughout scripture similar messages are presented in a variety of ways such as storytelling, letters or sermons. Relate Abigail's story of reconciliation to Paul's plea in II Corinthians 5:17-20. What is the common message in these two stories? How does Paul's message go beyond the story of Abigail?
- Suggest actual situations in our lives today that need to be reconciled (at the personal, national or global level). What kind of strategies could help to bring about reconciliation in any of these situations?

Creative Imagination

- Write a short play that dramatizes the interaction between Abigail and David that would reveal Abigail's strength of character and resourcefulness.
- Make a collage from magazine and newspaper articles to illustrate situations in the world that are in need of reconciliation.
- Choose a conflict situation from the modern world (countries at war, stand on abortion, ecology versus business, etc.). Role-play what both sides would be required to do to find a solution and be reconciled.
- Make a banner using symbols to represent acts of reconciliation.
- Other ideas....

Closing Ritual: Celebrating Biblical Women

Ask each person to bring a flower (real or artificial) or provide each person with a flower before starting the ritual.

Arrange chairs in a circle and set up a worship center on the floor or on a low table in the center. Use colourful cloths, candles, pictures of biblical women and a flower vase.

Explain the entire ritual in advance so no further instructions need to be given during the ritual.

Ask the participants to choose one biblical woman who has been an inspiration to them on their faith journey.

Explain that music will be played in order to give the participants time to make their choice and meditate on the significance of their biblical women.

Following the music, each person will come forward, name the woman, tell how and why she is an inspiration to them, and place a flower in the vase.

When each flower is placed in the vase participants will say the litany response: *For the inspiration she gives to us, we give thanks.*

Ritual

Music for meditation: Play a piece of quiet music.

Presentation of the flowers: Naming the woman describing her virtues, placing the flower in the vase, using the litany response.

Close the ritual by saying together:

As we go into the world
Living our daily lives,
May these women's stories inspire us
To be wise and courageous,
To speak with compassion,
To act with boldness
In God's work. Amen.

Huldah

So the priest Hilkiah, Ahikam, Achbor, Shaphan and Asaiah went to the prophetess Huldah.... II Kings 22:14a

Scripture Texts: *II Kings 22; 23:1-5, 21-25;*
II Chronicles 34.

Introduction

Most people have never heard of Huldah because she has been forgotten or ignored by church leaders. Many interpreters claim that she merely authenticated the Temple scroll as old and genuine. However, she did much more than that. She interpreted the text and proclaimed a prophetic warning from it. As an advisor to King Josiah she was able to influence his decisions, causing him to purify the Hebrew religion and reinstate ancient Hebrew rites. She would prove to be one of Israel's saviour figures.

Step I: Getting Acquainted with the Text

1. Read II Kings 22; 23:1-5, 21-25 silently and then choose a participant to read it aloud. On a flip chart record the sequence of events.
2. Read II Chronicles 34 in the same way. List the sequence of events and then compare this account to the one recorded in II Kings 22 and 23.
3. Share your general impressions or immediate response to the passages.
4. Write down any questions that may arise from the initial reading. Look for the answers as you complete the study.

Step II: Understanding the Text

1. Literary Form

After the fall of Jerusalem, an author called the Deuteronomistic Historian wrote a history to celebrate Israel's past and provide a foundation for its future. Drawing upon earlier writings and oral traditions, the author wrote the history of Israel as a narrative that was full of drama and poetry. It emphasizes the orthodox position within the Hebrew religion that records the fidelity of God toward humanity despite its weaknesses and rebellions. Although it is only one interpretation of Israel's history, it became the moral authority for Israel's future and the inspiration for its belief in God. The Deuteronomistic Historian focused on Moses as Israel's most important prophet and leader. This historical account claimed that the Hebrews were chosen by Yahweh and given the responsibility to live in a covenantal relationship according to the laws revealed to them by God through Moses. The Deuteronomistic Historian emphasized the concept that goodness brings rewards, but sin brings punishment. Huldah's story is part of the Deuteronomistic History (II Kings 22-23).

Some years later an author called the Chronicler wrote another interpretation of Israel's history. It was a factual account rather than a narrative and focused on the achievements of David and the restoration of Israel. The Chronicler selected material from the Deuteronomistic History that supported his version of Israel's history. Sometimes he reorganized the material or supplemented it with information from other sources. It is significant that the Chronicler kept the story of Huldah as part of his history, although it was told somewhat differently.

There is another reference to Huldah in *Jewish Antiquities* written by Josephus, a first-century Jewish historian:

> In the eighteenth year of his reign, the high priest Hilkiah came across the sacred books of Moses that had been stored in the temple and forgotten. He gave them to a scribe, who read them to the king. When he heard what was written about those who transgressed the law, he tore his clothes and sent messengers to the prophetess, Huldah, imploring her to pray to God and appease His anger. Because their forefathers had sinned, Josiah feared that his people would be driven out of their own country and exiled to a foreign land. Huldah sent back word that the Deity had already passed sentence against them, and no supplications would be effective. Because of the virtues of Josiah, however, He would postpone the disasters until after his death.
> *Josephus: The Essential Writings*, Maier, p. 177.

- How do these accounts affirm Huldah's importance in Israel's history?

2. Word Study

nabi:

Nabi is the masculine form of the Hebrew word for prophet and *nabiah* is the feminine form. Authentic prophets in Israel were modeled after Moses. Read Deuteronomy 18:15-22. There are many prophets named in the Hebrew Bible, among them are Amos, Micah, Isaiah and Jeremiah.

- What are the main characteristics and duties of prophets in Hebrew scripture?

Prophets in the Hebrew Bible are not fortunetellers or wizards. In fact the religious leaders of Israel condemned such practices. Read Leviticus 19:31; 20:6 and II Kings 23:24.

- What responsibility do the leaders have in regard to mediums and wizards that mislead the people?

In scripture, prophetic speech is given in a formal, recognizable pattern beginning with the phrase, "Thus says the Lord." Look up several examples of this type of speech: II Kings 9:1-3, II Chronicles 34:23-24 and Isaiah 37:21-22.

- Why is it important to note that Huldah used this speech pattern?
- How does Huldah, in her role as prophet, compare with other prophets such as Isaiah and Jeremiah? Are there similarities in the way their stories are told? In thinking about your answer, consider the following passages:
  - King Hezekiah consults Isaiah: II Kings 19:1-7
  - King Josiah consults Huldah: II Kings 22:14-20
  - King Zedekiah consults Jeremiah: Jeremiah 38:14-18

- Discover the stories of other women identified as prophets in scripture:
  - Exodus 15:20-21
  - Judges 4:4-5
  - Isaiah 8:3
  - Joel 2:28-29; Acts 2:17-18
  - Luke 2:36-38
  - Acts 21:8-9

Torah:

Torah is the Hebrew word for law, direction or instruction. Hebrew literature teaches that God, through Moses, revealed the law by which the Hebrew people must live. It was the responsibility of the prophets to keep the requirements of the law before the people, to teach the law to the next generation, and to call the people to repent if they were not following God's way.

Baal:

Baal is the Hebrew word for master, lord or husband. Quite frequently it refers to any deity other than the God of Israel. From Hebrew scripture we learn that Baal was the god of the Canaanites, and that from time to time the Israelites also worshipped that god. The Hebrew prophets spoke out against this practice claiming that it kept the people from following the true God of Israel.

Asherah:

Asherah was the name given to a cult object made of wood (a pole) that represented the Canaanite goddess Asherah. She was considered to be the consort of Baal. She was also worshipped by the Israelites at various times in their history, but the prophets warned against such practices because they threatened the people's covenant with God.

3. Historical Context

Throughout their early history, Israel and Judah were minor nations struggling to survive in the midst of the great dynasties of Assyria, Babylon and Egypt. They struggled constantly to protect themselves from absorption by the customs and cultures of the more powerful nations that surrounded them. The people of these nations worshipped many gods. In contrast, the Hebrews professed to have a covenant with one God, Yahweh, rejecting all idolatrous practices associated with the worship of many gods. It was a challenge for the prophets to maintain the idea of the supremacy of God's covenant and laws against the pressures of a polytheistic environment. At times even kings had to be reminded that they were not above the law. Because they were responsible for leading the people, they too must live according to God's way. It was the prophet's task to constantly remind the Hebrews that they were promised a secure and prosperous future if they remembered their covenant with God and acted accordingly.

Step III: Interpreting the Text

- What is Huldah's background? What credentials does she have for being a prophet? Why did King Josiah send his top officials to Huldah? What significance might you attach to his decision to go to her?

- What religious observances from foreign countries were threatening the unique identity of the Hebrew people? Read: II Kings 23:1-14.
- What was the prophetic warning that Huldah gave to King Josiah?
- How do we know that Huldah spoke with authority?
- What kind of God is portrayed in this text? Why do you think God was portrayed in this way?

Step IV: Reclaiming the Scriptures for Today

- What can be learned from Huldah's story about the Hebrew way of life, their hopes for the future, and their relationship with God?
- What can be learned about women in ancient Israel?
- For whom might Huldah be a suitable role model? How would you describe her in today's context? E.g., Huldah is like....
- How can attempts to preserve a religion or a way of life result in restrictive and narrow attitudes?
- Why is it important that we not become exclusive in our beliefs to the extent that we reject other faith positions?
- How do other religions challenge us today?
- How can we uphold our own religion without condemning others?
- Huldah spoke out against the practices that were threatening the well-being of her society. Who are the prophetic voices in our midst today? What "warnings" do we need to hear and respond to in our global community?

Creative Imagination

- Write a poem or song about Huldah that celebrates who she was and what she did.
- Make the case (as in a court of law) that Huldah was an authentic prophet in the Mosaic tradition.
- Outside the walls of Jerusalem archeologists have uncovered Huldah's tomb. Write a tombstone epitaph for her.
- Write a short play to dramatize Huldah's story.
- Other ideas....

Closing Ritual: Listening to the Prophets

Before starting the ritual choose two participants to read the scriptures from Isaiah.

Leader: Introduce the first reading by saying to the group,
"God talks to the Hebrew people telling them it is not pious fasting that is important in their covenant relationship. God states what is really acceptable."
Reader 1: Isaiah 58:6-7.
Leader: Introduce the second reading by saying to the group: "God says if they do these things then they will prosper."
Reader 2: Isaiah 58:9-12.

Give out slips of paper and pencils. Ask the participants to write down a modern day prophetic warning and place it in the basket.

Pass the basket around the circle. Ask each participant to select one of the papers, read it aloud and pause for a short meditation before passing the basket to the next person.

Listen to or sing Carolyn McDade's *Creation of Peace*. (see Bibliography)

Close the ritual by saying together:

Have we heard? (pause)

Have we listened? (pause)

Will we respond? (pause)

Amen

Esther

> *Who knows? Perhaps you have come to royal dignity for just such a time as this.*
> *Esther 4:14b*

Scripture Texts: All of Esther, with a focus on Esther 4:1–17.

Introduction

The story of Esther was written not only to entertain its readers, but also to inspire them. It was written at a time when many Jews were living in foreign lands as an oppressed minority. The story provided an inspirational model for Jews who needed to know how to live productively among foreigners without denying their own heritage.

People are rarely able to radically change the social and political structures in which they are forced to live, but this does not mean that they should do nothing. Esther accepted her role within the patriarchal setting, but found ways to use what power she had to protect her people. She is portrayed as a saviour figure and as a paradigm for survival.

Esther's story emphasizes the importance of responding to a call for justice, preparing oneself for possible risks and taking action to bring about change. Her story illustrates how the work of God is accomplished through the partnership of humankind and the divine.

Step I: Getting Acquainted with the Text

1. In preparation for the session have participants read the entire book of Esther.
2. When the group meets, ask one person to provide a summary of the main events. A good summary can be found in *Miriam, Mary and Me* by Lois Miriam Wilson (see Bibliography).
3. Read the specific text (Esther 4:1–17) silently and then ask a participant

to read it aloud. Jot down any questions or special points of interest that might be helpful during the study.

Step II: Understanding the Text

1. Literary Form

The Hebrew Bible is a collection of three groups of texts—the Torah, the Prophets, and the Writings. The book of Esther is found among the Writings. Although it is not classified as history, it might possibly be linked to an historical account where some Jews in Persia were saved from annihilation, and a Jew named Marduka was given an official position in the court of King Xerxes I of Persia. It is an exciting story, embellished with rich images of the Persian court and filled with suspense and intrigue. As a narrative about a young girl who becomes a queen and saves her people, the book of Esther also has a legendary, fairy-tale quality.

The book of Esther was not readily accepted as a canonical text to be included in the Bible because, in its original version, it contained no mention of God, no prayers and no explicit teachings about Jewish law or the covenant. These elements are nevertheless apparent in some of the characters' speech and action (Esther 3:2-4; 4:14; 9:30-31). The book of Esther finally made canon because it contains instructions for the celebration of the festival of *Purim*, a very popular event in the Jewish year (Esther 9:18-32).

When the Hebrew scriptures were translated into Greek (the Septuagint, 270 BCE), several additions, such as the prayers of Mordecai and Esther, were made to enhance the religious content of the story. In Protestant editions of the Bible these additions are found in the Apocrypha, a collection of writings that existed outside canon, but were used by the early Christian church for teaching and inspiration. In Catholic editions of the Bible, these additions were integrated into the text of the book of Esther.

- Find examples of irony and humour in the story of Esther.
- Why is the choice of a woman as the hero of the story an especially appropriate paradigm for the powerless?

2. Word Study

eunuch: (Esther 4:5)

A eunuch is a man who has been castrated and set apart for a special task such as guarding the king's harem or managing the king's household, consequently acquiring authority and respect. In the story of Esther eunuchs served the Persian king as his personal attendants (Esther 1:10-11), as gatekeepers (2:21), as protectors of the harem (2:3,14) and as attendants for the queen (4:5-11). References are made to eunuchs in both the Hebrew scriptures and the New Testament (Jeremiah 38:7-13; Acts 8:26-38).

- How was the special attention of the eunuch, Hathach, beneficial to Esther?

Diaspora: (Esther 1:1)

The *Diaspora* refers to the dispersion of the Jews who were forced to live in foreign countries after their defeat by Babylon (and later by Rome) (Isaiah 11:11-12; James 1:1). Prophets used the threat of dispersion as a punishment for not following God's way (Ezekiel 22:13-15). The *Diaspora* also refers to the Jews who chose to emigrate to other countries. In the first century CE Jewish settlements could be found throughout the known world, in Egypt, Italy, Asia Minor and Mesopotamia (I Peter 1:1).

Purim: (Esther 9:18-32)

Purim is the holiday commemorating the deliverance of the Jews from the massacre that Haman, the king's high official, had planned. The festival was initiated during the *Diaspora*, but was brought to Jerusalem for all Jews to celebrate. The plural of *pur* (lot) is *purim*, meaning "lots" and refers to the lot cast by Haman to determine the date of the massacre. Purim is celebrated on the fourteenth of *Adar* (February or March) on the Jewish calendar, the date determined by Haman's lot. During this celebration young girls dress up as Esther and imagine that they have risked their lives to save their people, while boys dress up as Mordecai. Poppy seed cookies in the shape of ears (Haman's ears) are crushed and eaten to symbolize the defeat of Haman.

3. Historical Context

Esther's story is set in the fifth century BCE when the Jews, as a conquered people, were living in Persia under the rule of King Xerxes I (called King Ahasuerus in Esther). Living in the Diaspora was challenging for the Hebrew people. They no longer had access to their temple in Jerusalem, to their land or to the national institutions that could sustain and comfort them. As a minority they had little defense against persecution as illustrated by Haman's plot to rid his country of Jews because Mordecai refused to bow down to him. To preserve their religion and survive in a foreign land Jewish refugees needed inspirational stories for encouragement and guidance. The book of Esther provided examples of courage, steadfastness and success for Jews living as a minority in a strange land.

Step III: Interpreting the Text

- The development of Esther's character is central to the story. Describe the transformation that Esther experiences from the time she goes to the harem until she decides to approach the king with her request.
- What is the crisis that confronts Esther (Esther 3:1-6)? Is she in a position to do much about her situation? What are the risks involved?
- How did she prepare herself to take these risks? How did she involve her community? Describe both the rational and the emotional appeal that she makes. Why were both necessary?
- In what ways is Esther fit to be a model of hope for all Jews living in the Diaspora?
- As a saviour figure how does Esther bring salvation, not only to her own people but also to the King's court?
- One predominant theme of the book of Esther is the promise that the lowly position of the poor and oppressed will someday be reversed. This is a common theme in the Bible (Isaiah 65:17-25; Luke 1:51-53). Discuss how this theme is presented in the story of Esther. What other theological messages or understandings of God are found in the book of Esther?

Step IV: Reclaiming the Scriptures for Today

- Esther takes time to prepare herself for the task ahead of her. Why is this preparation important? What do you do to prepare yourself for the Christian life of love and justice?
- At the beginning of the story Esther has no power, but by claiming the power available to her she saves her people. How can this story help us to plan our response to the injustices of our present world?
- Give examples of present-day injustices that have been challenged by individuals who, through their actions, were able to change society?

Creative Imagination

- Learn more about *Purim* by inviting women from the local synagogue to speak to the group about the special foods and events related to the festival.
- Make a collection of newspaper stories depicting women and men who dare to speak out against injustice.
- Write a play about Esther that can be performed by children.
- Do a modern interpretation of the verse: *for just such a time as this* (Esther 4:14b) for a church banner.
- Other ideas....

Closing Ritual: The Power of One

Set up a small worship center on a low table or on the floor using bright cloths, a candle and a container with some small stones. Suggested music: Carolyn McDade's *Song of a River* (see Bibliography).

Leader: Jesus recognized and understood that people have a power within themselves to make things happen. On several occasions he said to people who had been healed: "Your faith has saved you." He also said: "If you love God and your neighbour as yourself you have brought the reign of God very close." He suggested that acts of love, compassion and justice were ways of being in partnership with God.

Leader: Hold up a small stone saying: "This stone will be a symbol of your power to bring about change."

While quiet music is playing, the leader invites the participants to take a stone from the container. The leader then asks them to take a moment to silently reflect on the story of Esther and on her actions.

The leader will then encourage the participants to think about one action they can take within the next few weeks that can make a difference in someone's life or in society; e.g., call a neglected friend, write a letter in support of a social or political cause such as the homeless, speak out, join a march, etc.

The leader will instruct the participants to make an offering of their stone to symbolically express their commitment to take action. To the sound of background music participants are invited to place their stone on the worship table when they feel ready to do so.

At the end of the music and when all have placed their stones on the table, the leader closes the ritual by saying:

May the courage of Esther
Be our inspiration
To hear and respond
To God's call
For justice in our world.
Amen.

Second Isaiah

Enlarge the site of your tent, and let the curtains of your habitations be stretched out. *Isaiah 54:2a*

Scripture Texts: Second Isaiah 40–55 with a focus on chapters 54-55.

Introduction

The book of Isaiah, which was written over a period of nearly two hundred years, has at least three authors who can be identified by their distinct literary styles and by the historical inferences in their writing. The authors make reference to the Assyrian threat after the fall of Samaria, to the fall of Jerusalem and the subsequent exile in Babylon, and to the time after the exile when King Cyrus permitted the Israelites to return to their homeland. Because earlier material was reworked and additions made, it is difficult to determine exactly which chapters each author wrote; however, scholars generally group the chapters as Isaiah I:1-39; Isaiah II:40-55 and Isaiah III:56-66.

The writings do not reveal much about their authors. We know that First Isaiah is a man referred to as the son of Amoz (Isaiah 1:1). Both Second and Third Isaiah have been written anonymously, so we do not know if they were written by men or by women. Over the years it has been our assumption that Second Isaiah was written by a man because men wrote so much of scripture. Yet it is not inconceivable that a woman could be the author of Second Isaiah. To verify such an hypothesis it will be necessary to look for evidence from both the biblical record and from sources outside the Bible.

- There is evidence from biblical sources that some Hebrew women did, in fact, hold important positions and made significant prophetic statements. Although there are only a few accounts that refer to such activities by women, the biblical record does not suggest that these activities were unusual or exceptional. Evidence of women's prophetic statements can be found in Exodus 15:20-21 (Miriam); Judges 4:4-10 (Deborah); I

Samuel 2:1-10 (Hannah) and II Kings 22:14-20 (Huldah).

- When Nebuchadnezzar destroyed Jerusalem and exiled the Hebrews to Babylon, only the educated élite was forced to go, and it is possible that Second Isaiah belonged to that aristocratic group (II Kings 24:11-16). The Hebrews lived in Babylon for almost fifty years and during this time Hebrew women were exposed to the traditional practices of Babylonian women. Their society had a long history of women's participation in temple cultic practices that had originated with nomadic tribal traditions, but continued to exist even as the institutions of Babylon became more stabilized. Both the temple and the palace operated schools for girls continuously from 1800 to 539 BCE which suggests certain women were well educated and capable of producing literary works. In fact there was a long tradition of women writers in Mesopotamia; for example Princess Enheduanna, the daughter of Sargon, wrote *The Exultation of Inanna* as early as 2200 BCE.
- Some Babylonian women also held the highly influential position of prophet. Sibyl, a semi legendary figure, was the initiator of a tradition of prophecy that flourished from the eighth to the sixth century BCE. Her inspired leadership gave rise to the sibylline books that developed a new literary response to history.
- Second Isaiah uses feminine imagery to describe Jerusalem, Babylon and God. Use of this kind of imagery may indicate that the poetry expresses the experience of a woman.

Step I: Getting Acquainted with the Text

1. In preparation for the session participants should read all the text attributed to Second Isaiah (40 to 55).
2. When the group meets, read the following chapters aloud: Isaiah 54 and 55.
3. Share your immediate response to the writings of Second Isaiah.

Step II: Understanding the Text

1. Literary Form

The poetry of Second Isaiah was written as a collection of oracles firstly to answer the people's questioning about the suffering they have experienced as exiles in Babylon, and secondly to restore hope and optimism as they look to their future.

Second Isaiah makes effective use of a literary device known as "reversals". For instance Isaiah 47 states that Babylon will be brought down from her position of power and wickedness, while in Isaiah 54 and 55 Jerusalem will be raised to a new position that promises a future full of joy and plenty.

The writings of Second Isaiah are noted for their positive use of both masculine and feminine imagery. By using this descriptive language and imagery, Second Isaiah creates a powerful message of hope and renewal for the Hebrew people and expresses it as an exquisite piece of poetry.

2. Word Study

Jerusalem/Zion and Babylon/Chaldea:
It was common in ancient times to describe cities in female terms. This practice originated from an ancient belief that a goddess was the guardian of the city's inhabitants.

- How was Babylon/Chaldea characterized by Second Isaiah? Read Isaiah 47: 1-11.
- How was Jerusalem/Zion characterized? Read Isaiah 40:1-2; 49:14-18; 51:17-23; 52:1-2 and 54:1-8.

concepts of God:
Second Isaiah liberates the scripture's predominately masculine concept of God as a father or a warrior figure by using a great variety of metaphors and images to describe God. These positive images, which are both masculine and feminine, reveal a God that is compassionate, dependable and close by. By using many images of God, Second Isaiah broadens the concept of God.

- Make a list of the images of God found in Second Isaiah: 40:11,28-29; 41:10-13; 42:14; 44:24-28; 45:22; 46:3-4; 49:14-18; 52:9-10; 54:4-8; and 55:6-8.

3. Historical Context

The destruction of Jerusalem and the temple was a devastating catastrophe for the people who were left behind in Judah as well as those who were sent into exile in Babylon. These events raised the question of how such a thing could happen to God's chosen people.

- What questions would the Israelites be asking about themselves and about God?

For the fifty years that the Israelites lived in exile, they were not able to perform the religious rites of their ancestors in their holy Temple in Jerusalem. As the Israelites were gradually assimilated into the Babylonian culture, there was concern that they would cease to exist as a distinct people. Second Isaiah wrote to reassure them of God's compassion and concern for their well-being. She wrote to give them hope for a better future, especially since Cyrus the Persian king had defeated Babylon and allowed the Israelites to return to their homeland.

Step III: Interpreting the Text

Living in exile created a new context for the Israelites' understanding of God. This new situation brought forth doubts and questions about their special status as God's people. Second Isaiah responds to the situation with encouraging words that combine traditional ideas with new concepts.

- Why did God permit the Israelites to suffer? Second Isaiah provides a traditional answer in 42:21-25, but also introduces a new idea about Jerusalem's suffering. Second Isaiah suggests that Jerusalem suffered doubly for her sins because God's punishing action against her would redeem all the nations 40:2; 42:6-7; 43:8-10; 49:6.
- With God no longer confined to the Temple in Jerusalem, Second Isaiah develops the idea of a universal God accessible to all people and nations 45:5-7; 45:22; 52:10.
- God will not be restricted to using only Israelites as agents for God's work of justice. Who does God use to liberate Israel from the Babylonians? Read 44:28; 45:1 and 13; 46:8-11.
- Compare Second Isaiah's universal concept of God to the ideas Jesus presents when he speaks with the woman at the well in John 4:19-24.

When the exiles left Babylon and returned to Jerusalem, they would meet the inhabitants who had been left behind. Second Isaiah was concerned that the exiles would not be well received; they might be perceived as foreigners because of their long connection with the Babylonians.

- How did Second Isaiah want those who were returning to feel about themselves? Read 54:4-8.

- How did she want Jerusalem to greet them? Read 54:2-3.
- What was God's promise for them on their return? Read 55.
- Imagine how the people would respond to the writings of Second Isaiah.

Step IV: Reclaiming the Scripture for Today

- Second Isaiah uses both feminine and masculine images to emphasize the universal, inclusiveness of God. Does the liturgy of our churches today reflect the inclusiveness of Second Isaiah's message? How can the use of feminine imagery in church liturgies contribute to the self worth of women?
- Third Isaiah continues to build on the ideas of Second Isaiah (Isaiah 56:1-8), but others such as Ezra (Ezra 9:1-4) and Nehemiah (Nehemiah 13:1-3 and 23-27) advocate that their religion be purified. How can the purification of religious practices and beliefs lead to racism?
- Racism is a problem throughout the world as well as in our own country. Discuss the effects of racism on individuals and on communities. What effect does it have on both the victims and the perpetrators? (see Bibliography)
- By developing the concept of a universal God who cares about all people (not just the Israelites), how do the writings of Second Isaiah challenge us to end racism?
- How can the poetry of Second Isaiah encourage and inspire people to celebrate their religious, cultural and ethnic differences?
- Do you agree or disagree with Second Isaiah's optimism about what God can do? Explain why or why not.

Creative Imagination

- Write a poem about your relationship with God.
- With Second Isaiah as inspiration, write a litany that would give hope to a world in crisis.
- Plan a "poetry reading" event to share what the group has written.
- Research the work of modern day poets such as Joyce Rupp (*Prayers to Sophia*), Miriam Therese Winter (*WomanWisdom*) and Keri Wehlander (*Circles of Grace*) who write inspirational poetry for individual use or group gatherings.
- Use the images in one of Second Isaiah's poems to create a wall hanging. Use cloth, paper, felt or other mediums. Isaiah 40:28-31; 41:17-20; or 49:13.

- Write a song to honour women poets, prophets and writers from ancient Israel. (You might use a familiar tune in the same way the Raging Grannies create a social justice song.)
- Other....

Closing Ritual: Reaching Out

Gather symbols of hope and inclusiveness and place them on a small table in the center of the circle.

Read together Miriam Therese Winter's poem based on Isaiah 54 "A Psalm to Widen Our Tents." Instruct half the group to be Choir I and the other half to be Choir II with the whole group being All.

Play music and give the participants a few moments to choose one part of the poem that speaks to them. Ask the participants to tell why their selection is meaningful to them.

Close the ritual by asking the participants to read the poem once more.

A Psalm to Widen Our Tents

Choir 1 Our world is too small,
Our lives are too small,
Our vision is too restricted.

Choir 2 May the people of various countries,
various cultures, tribes and families
find room in our world and our lives.

All Help us to widen our tents, Shaddai,
so that all are welcome among us.

Choir 1 Our attitudes are too parochial,
our assumptions too simplistic,
our behavior too predictable.

Choir 2 May special people,
may the differently abled,
may minorities of any kind–
of race, class or gender–
find room in our world and in our hearts.

All Help us to widen our tents, Shaddai,
so that all are welcome among us.

Choir 1 Our boundaries are too limited,
our preferences too conditioned,
our habits too ingrained.

Choir 2 May the aging and the very young,
may subcultural groups of every kind
may special interest caucuses
find room in our world and our prayer.

All Help us to widen our tents, Shaddai,
so that all are welcome among us.

Choir 1 Our God is too small.
Our rites are too rigid.
Our ways are too exclusive.

Choir 2 May people of various religions and rites,
whose name for God and claim to God
are different from our own,
find room in our world and our love.

All Help us to widen our tents, Shaddai,
so that all are welcome among us.

"A Psalm to Widen Our Tents", from the book, *WomanWisdom* by Miriam Therese Winter, ©Medical Mission Sisters, 1991.

Mary: The Mother Of Jesus

All these were constantly devoting themselves to prayer, together with certain women, including Mary the mother of Jesus, as well as his brothers.
Acts 1:14

Scripture Texts: *The Birth Narrative: Matthew 1:18–2:23; Luke 1:26–2:20; Mary as mother: Matthew 13:54–56; Luke 2:21–51; Mary as disciple and God's agent: Luke 1:38, 46–55; John 2:1–12; 19:25–27; Acts 1:14; 2:1–4.*

Introduction

There is surprisingly little information about Mary in scripture, and most of it cannot be considered historical. Our image of Mary has been formed by various interpretations of the birth narratives in Matthew and Luke, as well as by church traditions that have evolved throughout the centuries. Tradition has focused on Mary as the mother of Jesus; however, a careful reading of the texts reveals that Mary was active in many other ways. There is evidence that she played a significant role in the salvation history of Israel, both as a disciple of Jesus in the new community and as God's agent. Scholars have done a considerable amount of work to search for the historical Jesus. This study will focus on the search for the biblical Mary.

Step I: Getting Acquainted with the Text

1. Organize the participants into two groups. Ask one group to research the birth narrative in Matthew, and the other the birth story in Luke. Participants are to answer the following questions and record the main points on a flip chart.

    - What are the key events in the story?
    - Who is the main character?
    - How is Mary portrayed?

2. Have each group report on its research and answer the following questions.

   - What is similar about these two stories? How do they differ?
   - Many people want to harmonize the two narratives from Matthew and Luke into one historical account of Jesus' birth. Why is this difficult to do? Name one sequence of events that cannot be harmonized.
   - What conclusions can be drawn about the birth of Jesus from these two accounts?

Step II: Understanding the Text

1. Literary Form

Matthew and Luke both use a variety of literary forms to tell the birth narrative. Let us look at a few.

- Both birth stories are "confessional" narratives because they express what the church community believed after the resurrection of Jesus—that Jesus is the Son of God who comes from God through virginal birth. The stories were written retroactively to proclaim the uniqueness of Jesus.

- Matthew and Luke use two literary techniques found frequently in the Hebrew scriptures—the "proclamation" formula and the "call" formula. In the "proclamation" formula a heavenly being appears to announce the birth of a son. The child is given a name and his future is revealed. Identify the formula in Genesis 16:7–12 as well as the birth stories of both John the Baptist (Luke 1:5–20) and Jesus (Luke 1:26–33).

- In the "call" formula God calls a person to be an agent for God. The recipient of the "call' expresses doubt that she or he will be able to respond adequately. God removes the doubt with the assurance that the Divine presence will not abandon the agent and will provide a sign as proof. Compare Moses' "call" formula (Exodus 3:7–12) with the one used to tell Mary's story (Luke 1:26–38). What other figures in scripture received a similar call?

- Luke places a canticle on the lips of Mary which today is known as the Magnificat (Luke 1:46–55). It is similar to Hannah's prayer (I Samuel 2:1–10). The canticle contains a literary technique called a "reversal" that is widely used in scripture. A "reversal" describes a change of fortune where the mighty are brought down and the lowly are raised. It is used to describe God's saving power for the world. Second Isaiah uses this technique to show how God can change the fortunes of Jerusalem (Isaiah 47:1–4 and 52:1-2).

Other appearances of Mary in scripture are limited to short references about her involvement with Jesus and his community.

2. Word Study

virgin:
Ordinarily this word referred to a young woman who was not yet married. Her virginity would end when she conceived a child. When Matthew describes Mary as a virgin, he is referring to the text of Isaiah 7:14 (Matthew 1:22–23) as proof that Jesus was the fulfillment of an ancient prophecy about a Messiah who was to come to redeem Israel. Isaiah's original prophecy, however, was concerned with the immediate future of Israel, not with a Messiah that would come several hundred years later. Matthew combined Isaiah's prophecy with the idea that Mary's conception of Jesus was from the Holy Spirit and not from Joseph. Luke also suggests that Mary conceived as a virgin without male sperm. Although biologically impossible, Matthew and Luke both use virginal conception to explain Jesus' birth. Greco-Roman religions contain many stories about male gods mating with mortal women. Caesar Augustus' mother was believed to have been visited by a serpent when she conceived him. The births of Hebrew patriarchs were often described as God's miracle when women were barren or too old to conceive (Genesis 17:15–19 and Judges 13:2–3, 24).

- How is Mary's conception similar yet different from other accounts of miraculous births?
- Give reasons to explain why Matthew and Luke chose to portray Jesus' birth as virginal?

maidservant/slave: (Luke 1:38)
The Greek word *doulos* is properly translated as "slave", as well as servant, because it signifies that a person has willingly and completely given herself or himself to God. This word is used to describe the prophets of the Hebrew scriptures (Jeremiah 25:4; Amos 3:7) as well as the apostles (Acts 4:29-30) and even Paul (Romans 1:1). *Doulos* was not used to denigrate or demean a

person or to describe passive behaviour, but rather was an important and significant title for true believers who were actively involved in the world as God's agents. At the same time, however, the term expresses the idea of humility in the presence of a higher power.

3. Historical Context

The authors who wrote about Jesus were responding to their respective communities. Paul's writings, the earliest we have about Jesus, do not include an account of Jesus' life or ministry. Paul's only reference to Jesus' birth states that he was "born of a woman" (Galatians 4:4–5). Paul's emphasis was to define and explain the theological significance of Jesus as the Son of God who was exalted to glory through the resurrection, not through his birth. When Mark wrote his gospel he also made no reference to Jesus' birth. Instead his gospel emphasized faithfulness to Jesus' message and to his new community. By the time the gospels of Matthew, Luke and John were written there was a growing need to stress the authenticity of Jesus as the true Messiah and to affirm the inclusiveness of both Jews and Gentiles among his followers. As Christianity spread throughout the Mediterranean it had to confront increased opposition from devout Jews who did not believe that Jesus was the long awaited Messiah. Followers of Christianity also suffered discrimination and oppression by Gentiles who felt that Christian teachings challenged the societal structures of Rome, especially family life. These authors wrote for an audience that needed to be reassured about the foundations of their faith so they could withstand the growing opposition to their beliefs and practices.

Step III: Interpreting the Text

The Annunciation

Mary was betrothed to Joseph, but she became pregnant before she married him. Because most people today reject the literal interpretation that she was impregnated by the Holy Spirit without human sperm, questions have arisen about what really happened.

In spite of the biblical record, many believe that Joseph was the natural father. Some scholars suggest that Matthew and Luke were attempting to explain away a scandalous rumour that Jesus' birth was the result of an act of adultery or rape. These scholars argue, that despite this situation, the baby born to Mary was recognized as God's son and the long awaited Messiah.

- If the scholars are correct and Jesus was illegitimate, what is this story telling us about God and about who can be a saviour figure for the Hebrew people?
- There are four women inserted into Matthew's genealogy of Jesus—Tamar, Rahab, Ruth and the wife of Uriah, Bathsheba (Matthew 1:2-6). All four of these women acted as God's agents in their search for justice. How is God's choice of Mary as an agent consistent with the choice of these four women?

Other scholars argue that Jesus' birth story is similar to all miraculous birth stories written about powerful people in the ancient world. The concept of a virginal birth by the Holy Spirit portrays Jesus' birth as greater than any other birth in Jewish or Roman writings. It challenges the uniqueness of even the Emperor of Rome who was conceived with the mediation of a serpent.

- What political statement were Matthew and Luke making about Jesus' birth and his power to change the world?
- What other suggestions would you make to explain the idea of a virgin birth?

The Magnificat: (Luke 1:46–55)

- What is the essence of this poetic hymn of praise?
- How might the Romans interpret this hymn?
- What does this hymn tell us about Luke's understanding of Mary?
- Relate the Magnificat to the reading given by Jesus in the synagogue when he began his ministry (Luke 4:16–28). What response did Jesus receive from his audience?

Mary's Visit with Elizabeth: (Luke 1:39–56)

When they are both pregnant, Mary goes to stay with the aging Elizabeth. This story about the coming of a saviour who will redeem Israel and change the world is rich in metaphorical meaning.

- How is each woman part of the change that is about to take place in the world?
- How does the conversation of Mary and Elizabeth provide insights into the future ministry of Jesus?
- What is God's role in this visitation?

Mary as mother: (Matthew 13:54–56; Luke 2:21–24, 41–51; John 2:1–12)

- How is Mary portrayed as a mother figure in these texts?
- What other family did Mary have after the birth of Jesus?
- How did she show concern for Jesus as he developed his ministry?

Mary as disciple and agent of God:
According to the gospel message, an ideal disciple was one who heard the word of God and acted upon it (Luke 8:21). Hebrew scripture uses the phrase "blessed are you among women" to describe women who helped to save God's people from destruction (Judges 5:24; Judith 13:18-20). Mary is also addressed in this way (Luke 1:42–45).

- How does Luke's story of the visitation of Elizabeth and Mary confirm the idea that Mary was a disciple?
- What did Mary learn from Jesus about being a disciple in his new community (Mark 3:31–35)?
- How did she express her loyalty and faith in Jesus and in his ministry (John 2:1-12; 19:25-27; Acts 1:14; 2:1–4)?
- Having gathered all this information, what is your impression of Mary? What words would you use to describe her qualities?

Step IV: Reclaiming the Scripture for Today

Over the centuries the church's portrayal of Mary has gone far beyond what is recorded about her in scripture. Tradition has made her pure, sexless and sinless. Her many titles include "perpetual virgin", *Theotokos* (Mother of God), compassionate mediator for the people, and healer. Claims are made that she has been lifted up into heaven, and that she appears even today to people around the world.

- Where do you think these non-scriptural ideas come from?
- How does your church community understand Mary? Do you agree with this assessment of who she was and what she did?
- Some people feel that the tradition which names Mary as sinless and sexless has been harmful to women and to their self image, particularly when Mary is upheld as a model for all women to emulate. Can the church's traditional image of Mary be a model for women today? Give reasons for your opinion.

- In what way might Mary be a role model?

While some view Mary as a feminine expression of the Divine, others argue that she has been put on too high a pedestal.

- What are your feelings about Mary?
- How would you like to see her portrayed?

Creative Imagination

- Write a birth narrative from Mary's perspective that would reveal her thoughts and concerns about her role as God's agent in salvation history.
- Create a banner to depict Mary as a disciple.
- Write a litany to celebrate Mary in a way that is meaningful to you or to your group.
- Gather pictures, icons, figurines, etc. from over the centuries and discuss the various ways that Mary has been understood.
- Other ideas....

Closing Ritual: Celebrating Mary

Before the ritual begins assign the parts for the play. Preparation beforehand will help to make it a lively dramatic presentation.

Set up a meditation center using pictures and icons that represent Mary's role in God's saving acts.

Play the music, "Ave Maria" or the "Magnificat."

Read the play (see below) written by the people of South America.

Close by saying together:

Walk with Mary
The path of discipleship
Proclaiming the good news
Of justice for the poor and homeless.
Share her praise
Of the Divine
That calls us forth to do God's work.
Walk with Mary
In hope. Amen

"The Play" about Mary

PRIEST: Today is September 12. Does that date mean anything special to you?
RESPONSE: Three years ago yesterday Allende was killed in Chile and the Chileans lost their leader. Now they are suffering repression.
RESPONSE: Allende's death makes me think of the death of Martin Luther King.
PRIEST: Why do you think of the deaths of those two together?
RESPONSE: Because both of them were concerned about oppressed peoples.
PRIEST: Doesn't the day mean anything but *death* to you?
RESPONSE: Well, today is also the Feast of the Holy Name of Mary. So this day also makes me think of her.
PRIEST: Is there any connection between Allende and Martin Luther King and Mary?
RESPONSE: I guess that would depend on whether Mary was concerned about oppressed peoples too.
PRIEST: Let me read part of Mary's song, the Magnificat, in the beginning of Luke's Gospel: "God has scattered the proud in the imagination of their hearts, put down the mighty from their thrones, and exalted those of low degree; has filled the hungry with good things, and the rich has sent empty away."
RESPONSE: Bravo! But, Father, that doesn't sound at all like the Mary we hear about in the cathedral. And the Mary in the "holy pictures" certainly doesn't look like a person who would talk that way.
PRIEST: Tell us about the Mary in the holy pictures.
RESPONSE *(displaying a picture)*: Here she is. She is standing on a crescent moon. She is wearing a crown. She has rings on her fingers. She has a blue robe embroidered with gold.
PRIEST: That *does* sound like a different Mary from the Mary of the song! Do you think the picture has betrayed the Mary of the song?
RESPONSE: The Mary who said that God "has exalted those of low degree" would not have left all of her friends so she could stand on the moon.
CORPORATE RESPONSE: Take her off the moon!
RESPONSE: The Mary who said that God "has put down the mighty from their thrones" would not be wearing a crown.
CORPORATE RESPONSE: Take off her crown!
RESPONSE: The Mary who said that God "has sent the rich empty away" would not be wearing rings on her fingers.
CORPORATE RESPONSE: Take off her rings!

RESPONSE: The Mary who said that God has "filled the hungry with good things" would not have left people who were still hungry to wear a silk robe embroidered with gold.
CORPORATE RESPONSE: Take off her robe!
ANGUISHED RESPONSE: But, Father, this is not right! *(embarrassedly)* We're—we're doing a striptease of the Virgin.
PRIEST: Very well. If you don't like the way Mary looks in this picture, what do you think the Mary of the song would look like?
RESPONSE: The Mary of the song would not be standing on the moon. She would be standing in the dirt and dust where we stand.
RESPONSE: The Mary of the song would not be wearing a crown. She would have on an old hat like the rest of us, to keep the sun from causing her to faint.
RESPONSE: The Mary of the song would not be wearing jeweled rings on her fingers. She would have rough hands like ours.
RESPONSE: The Mary of the song would not be wearing a silk robe embroidered with gold. She would be wearing old clothes like the rest of us.
EMBARRASSED RESPONSE: Father, it may be awful to say this, but it sounds as though Mary would look just like me! My feet are dirty, my hat is old, my hands are rough, and my clothes are torn.
PRIEST: No, I don't think it is awful to say that. I think the Mary you have all described is more like the Mary of the Bible than the Mary we hear about in the cathedral and see in all the holy pictures.
RESPONSE: I think she'd be more at home here in the slum with us than in the cathedral or the General's Mansion.
RESPONSE: I think her message is more hopeful for us than for them. They are mighty and rich, but she tells them that God puts down the mighty from their thrones and sends the rich away empty.
RESPONSE: And we are at the bottom of the heap and very hungry, but she tells us that God exalts those of low degree and fills the hungry with good things.
PRIEST: Now let's see, how could we begin to help God bring those things to pass?

Brown, Robert McAfee, *Unexpected News: Reading the Bible with Third World Eyes.* Philadelphia: Westminster Press, 1984.

Anna

At that moment she came, and began to praise God and to speak about the child to all who were looking for the redemption of Jerusalem.

Luke 2:38

Scripture Texts: *Luke 2:36–38;*
I Timothy 5:3–16.

Introduction

Although Luke is the only gospel writer to mention Anna, and although there are only four sentences about her, this short passage can nevertheless be useful for a greater understanding of the ministry of women in the early Christian community. It provides a considerable amount of information about Anna, her strong Jewish heritage, her faithfulness to her religion and her ministry of proclamation.

In addition to being named a prophet, Anna is identified as a widow. In Hebrew society widows were in an economically and socially precarious position and were therefore thought to be in the special care of God. The church believed that the prayers of widows were more likely to be heard by God than any others. Because of the communal nature of the early church, widows were well cared for and they were not left destitute and alone. It appears that for a time in the early Christian church widows gathered as a special group within the community and may have functioned as an "Order of Widows." As part of this "Order", widows had specific duties to perform on behalf of the congregation. These special groups of widows with their specific duties did not survive beyond the third century. An emerging church hierarchy began to determine who could hold office in the evolving church structure and what kinds of activities women would be permitted to do.

This study will be carried out in two parts. Part I will focus on Anna, who she was and why she is important (Luke 2:36-38). Part II will focus on the widows of the early Christian church, who they were and what they did (I Timothy 5:3-16).

Part I of Anna: (Luke 2:36-38)

Step I: Getting Acquainted with the Text

1. Read the text silently and then ask a participant to read it aloud.
2. What is your immediate response to the text?

Step II: Understanding the Text

1. Literary Form

Anna's story is a short scenario within the larger birth narrative of Luke's gospel. Luke used an interesting technique when writing his gospel - he told the stories of men and women in pairs. Examples can be found in chapters 7,8,13 and 15.

- Read the account about Simeon who is coupled with Anna (Luke 2:25-35). How much more has been told about Simeon than about Anna? How do Simeon and Anna reflect the inclusiveness of Luke's message?

2. Word Study

widow:
The Hebrew word for widow is *almanah*, which is derived from the same root as muteness, expressing silence or an inability to speak. The word is associated with one who is helpless and oppressed and consequently comes under the special care of God (Psalm 68:5 and 146:9). Many times in the Hebrew scriptures references are made about the people's responsibility to take care of the widows (Deuteronomy 14:28-29 and Jeremiah 7:5–7).

of the tribe of Asher:
Luke identifies Anna's origin as the tribe of Asher, one of the twelve tribes of Israel that held land as their inheritance (Joshua 19:24–31). Her tribe was one of the "ten lost tribes" of Israel that disappeared after the Assyrian destruction of Samaria. Luke's reference to Anna's heritage may suggest that descendents of the "lost" tribe still existed and were connected to the Temple in Jerusalem.

3. Historical Context

Luke's gospel was written in the latter part of the first century. In many ways Luke wrote as an apologist for the truth claims that were being circulated about Jesus as the Christ. It was important for Luke to establish a strong connection between Jesus and the earlier Jewish expectations of a Messiah that will redeem Israel. The story of Anna helps to make this connection by linking her with an ancient Hebrew tribe that remained a part of Israel. Luke also had to be concerned with the growing number of non-Jews who were being attracted to Christianity. He needed to emphasize the inclusiveness of Jesus' message.

Step III: Interpreting the text

- Who is Anna? What information connects her to her Hebrew past? Why is it important to know her family connections?
- What is her spiritual task in the Temple? Why is she part of the Temple establishment?
- What is she concerned about?
- What public announcement does she make? Does her announcement sound "revolutionary"?
- Luke also refers to widows in Acts 6:1–6. What problem is expressed in this text? How is it resolved? Why is this ministry to widows so important?

Part II of Anna: (I Timothy 5:3-16)

Step I: Getting Acquainted with the Text

1. Read the text silently and then ask a participant to read it aloud.
2. Describe your immediate response to the text.
3. Does the content of the text cause any uneasiness? If so, explain why.

Step II: Understanding the Text

1. Literary Form

I Timothy is one of three "letters" (I and II Timothy, and Titus) entitled the Pastoral Epistles. Scholars suggest that these writings are more like a handbook of instructions for a church community than true letters. After intensive study of these writings, scholars have concluded that the letters were not written by Paul the Apostle, but were attributed to him to establish their authority in giving advice. The writing style of the Pastoral Epistles is not the same as that found in Paul's other letters that are known to be authentic, nor is the theological content compatible with the ideas found in Paul's true writings. Scholars note that the description of the church's hierarchical structure in these letters reflect developments that would not have been present in Paul's day. For instance, the inequality between men and women did not exist in Paul's church, but belongs to a time when women's roles as church leaders were being threatened. As a result of these differences, scholars have concluded that these letters were written circa 125 CE after Paul's death. The overall intention of these letters was meant to inspire and encourage the young church to preserve the faith and to protect its teachings from heresy.

2. Word Study

real widow: (I Timothy 5:3-8)
The Greek word for widow is *chera*. Like the Hebrew word, it is connected to the idea of a person in need. The concept of being a "real widow" points to a special class of women within the Christian community to which every woman could belong if she fulfilled certain requirements. According to the letter to Timothy, this position also came with certain privileges and responsibilities. The community would care for widows, only if family members were unable to care for them.

first pledge: (I Timothy 5:11-12)
Women who were put on the list of "real" widows had to make a vow or pledge to uphold and maintain the requirements of being a "real" widow. Vows were taken seriously and not easily broken.

- Which women were more likely to break these pledges? For what reason? Why was this a problem?

3. Historical Context

The letter sent to Timothy was written in the historical context of the year 125 CE. A great many changes have occurred since the beginnings of the Christian church at Pentecost. What began as a Jewish movement had quickly developed into a predominately Gentile one. During this early period of church development there were many interpretations of the life and teachings about Jesus as the Christ. Concern grew among certain church leaders that there was too much diversity, and they feared that the "original" teachings would be lost. It was felt that church doctrine and hierarchical authority must be developed to protect the church against heresy. During these first hundred years the Christian movement spread to many parts of the Mediterranean where it encountered the ideas and norms of the powerful Roman Empire. Rome was the model for a hierarchical structuring of society, including both the state and the family household. As a minority religion, Christian communities began to feel the need to conform to the Roman way of life and to gain respectability among their neighbours to avoid persecution. Women and their roles in the ministry of the church were adversely affected by these concerns.

Step III: Interpreting the Text

In the Pastoral Letter of I Timothy reference is made to the existence of a particular group of women known as widows. They were celibate, lived in communities with each other and held a variety of leadership roles in the ministry of the church. Anna, as a prophet who could make a proclamation, stands out as an example of this early ministry where women had some authority to speak. However, the author of I Timothy wants to reduce the role of these widows in the hierarchical church and sets out in his letter rules and regulations to limit their involvement and activities. By the third century this group of widows had completely disappeared.

- What are the requirements for being accepted as a "real" widow (I Timothy 5:9–10)?
- What activities may "real" widows carry out in their service to the church? Why might Anna be considered a "real" widow? How did her activities go beyond the role of a "real" widow?
- What advice does the author give concerning the status of younger women? What concerns him about their behaviour? How might these activities be perceived as a threat to the developing church hierarchy?
- Who should care for the widows? Why should it be their responsibility (I Timothy 5:4-8)? How does this new requirement compare to Luke's account of caring for widows (Acts 6:1–6)?
- From all that you have read about the widows would you agree with those scholars who argue that there was an "Order of Widows" during the early church's ministry? Give reasons for your answer.

Parts I and II: Reclaiming the Scripture for Today

- Why could the "Order of Widows" not survive beyond the third century? What distinct women's groups did survive? How were they similar to the "Order of Widows"? How were they different?
- What is the situation of widows today, both in society and in the church?
- How can the church and society be supportive and inclusive of widows?
- What special abilities and attitudes might today's widows bring to the ministry of the church if they are supported and encouraged?
- The early church and its development is a fertile ground for further research. Why would this research be particularly important to women?

Creative Imagination

- Write a prayer that Anna might have spoken in the Temple.
- Envision a possible "Order of Widows" as it may have functioned in the first century. Envision a similar "Order of Widows" that might exist today. Who would they be? What might they do? How might they relate to each other?
- Write a ritual to honour widows in our church today.
- Arrange a gathering where widows could discuss their particular concerns and suggest ways how the church might respond.
- Other....

Closing Ritual: Honouring our Ancestors

Prepare a ritual center using candles or flowers and bright-coloured cloths and place it in the center of a circle of chairs.

Ask the participants to bring a photograph of their mother or grandmother.

Ask the participants to tell an anecdotal story about their relative and why she was special to them. Place each photo on the ritual table before the next story is told.

Close the ritual by saying:

We honour our ancestors
Who gave life to us.
We give thanks
For their wisdom, their loving care
And their visions for life. Amen

Mary Magdalene

Mary Magdalene went and announced to the disciples, "I have seen the Lord"; and she told them that he had said these things to her. John 20:18

Scripture Texts: *Matthew 27:55-61; 28:1-10, 16;*
Mark 15:40–41, 47; 16:1–9;
Luke 8:1–3; 23:49, 55–56; 24:1–11, 22;
John 19:25; 20:11–18.

Introduction

The figure of Mary Magdalene arouses our curiosity, for while she is acclaimed in all four gospels as the principle witness to the death and resurrection of Jesus, the church has never portrayed her as equal in status to either Peter or Paul. The church has chosen to ignore her close connection to Jesus, her active participation in the movement, and her willingness to take the necessary risks in support of Jesus' ministry.

The medieval church glorified Mary Magdalene as a saint, not because of her role as witness and messenger of the good news, but because she was a "penitent whore". The church portrayed her as a prostitute whose sin was forgiven by Christ. The religious focus of church leaders during the Middle Ages emphasized sin, guilt and salvation and they used Mary Magdalene as a model for those who had sinned and were seeking redemption. They portrayed Mary Magdalene as a composite of all the women of the gospels who were perceived as sinners(the woman who washed Jesus' feet (Luke 7:36-50), the adulteress who was brought before Jesus to be condemned (John 8:1-11), and even the woman at the well (John 4:7-18).

Other references to Mary Magdalene in both Mark and Luke's gospels describe her as one of the women who took part in Jesus' itinerant ministry, not only participating as a close follower, but as a patron or benefactor who supported his ministry financially.

It is time for the church to restore Mary Magdalene to her rightful position as a major figure in the formation and development of the Christian community. Her contribution is well documented in the gospel accounts. This study is designed to examine anew the life and contribution of Mary Magdalene, and in the process it may exonerate her and give her the recognition she deserves.

Step I: Getting Acquainted with the Text

- Before reading the biblical texts, prepare a chart on a large piece of paper to record the information that is available about Mary Magdalene in the gospels. Divide the chart into four columns and respectively label them Mark, Matthew, Luke and John.
- Start by reading aloud the specified texts from Mark, considered to be the earliest gospel writer (circa 60 CE). Note, however, that verses 9-20 in chapter 16 are thought to be later additions because they do not appear in the earlier versions of the gospel. Ask participants to identify information and record it on the chart.
- Read aloud the listed texts from Matthew, Luke and John and ask participants to identify and record relevant information on the chart. When writing down the information, use an "S" to indicate that the detail is similar to Mark and a "D" to indicate that it is different.
- Hang the chart where it can be seen so the group can refer to it again later in the study.

Step II: Understanding the Text

1. Literary Form

As the chart that was prepared in the previous section makes clear, the stories of the four gospels are not always consistent in describing Mary Magdalene, especially in connection to the crucifixion and resurrection of Jesus. Readers must remember that each gospel writer worked from several sources and carefully selected details that would support a particular point of view and the needs of the community for which the authors wrote.

Mark's gospel is particularly interesting to examine. The original ending suggests that the women told no one what they had seen or heard about the resurrection. In a dramatic final scene it appears that everyone, the male disciples and even the faithful women, had deserted Jesus. One has to speculate about why Mark chose to end the gospel this way. All four gospels use literary techniques to draw listeners into the story, forcing them to make some decisions of their own. The gospels were written in an era of persecution when followers needed to be encouraged to keep the faith and trust that Jesus was truly the Messiah. Could Mark possibly have been challenging his community not to deny Jesus as the characters in the story did?

2. Word Study

Magdalene:
The meaning of "Magdalene" is not entirely clear. There are several possibilities for its translation. Magdalene may indicate Mary Magdalene's city of origin, Magdala, a wealthy fishing village on the north-west bank of the Sea of Galilee. Magdala was notorious for its prostitution and licentious living. Did Mary Magdalene come from this notorious village and was she therefore a prostitute? Other scholars relate Magdalene to the Hebrew word *migdal* that refers to a tower or a stronghold, a symbol of strength and protection. In 412 St. Jerome referred to Mary Magdalene in one of his letters as the one who was called the tower because she was strong in her faith. In that reference Magdalene seems to have been used as an adjective to describe her character. Unlike the other gospel writers who describe Mary Magdalene as a woman from Magdala, Luke refers to her as Mary, the one called Magdalene (Luke 8:2).

apostle:
The word apostle appears in different forms in the gospel texts. As a Greek noun *apostolos* refers to a delegate, an ambassador or a messenger. As a verb *apostello* means "to send out." In general biblical usage the word denotes anyone who proclaimed the gospel. A number of people such as Barnabas (Acts 14:14), Andronicus and Junia (Romans 16:7), Paul (I Corinthians 1:1) and James, Jesus' brother (Galatians 1:18-19) are identified as apostles. A more restrictive use of the word was applied to a select group of highly honoured believers such as the Twelve Disciples. As part of the evolving church, this office was upheld as the most important of the spiritual gifts (I Corinthians 12:28). Although some people were not specifically named as apostles in scripture, their actions fulfilled the general description of the role. Mary Magdalene was commissioned by Jesus to tell others what she had seen and heard, and so she became a messenger for him. In a similar way the Samaritan woman at the well was also the messenger of the good news.

sinner:
The dictionary meaning of the biblical word *sinner* denotes a person who is unfaithful to God, a person not fulfilling the religious requirements, or someone outside the Hebrew faith and its practices such as a heathen or a Gentile. A person who is called a *sinner* may or may not be a prostitute or a sexually immoral person. If the Greek word for prostitute (*pornos*) is not specifically used, then other information in the text needs to be considered to determine what kind of sinner is being described.

For many years Mary Magdalene has been equated with the woman in Luke 7:37. This text states that a woman in the city, a sinner, washed Jesus' feet with her tears and her hair, but it does not state the nature of her sin. Interpreters have suggested that she was a prostitute because her hair was loose and long enough to wipe Jesus' feet. She did not behave and dress like a respectable woman who would have covered her head. There is no evidence to suggest a connection between this sinner and Mary Magdalene, but Church Fathers such as Pope Gregory the Great declared that they were the same person.

3. Historical Context

In a patriarchal society women were not free to function publicly in the same way that men could. Scholars have questioned whether Mary Magdalene's participation in Jesus' itinerant ministry was socially acceptable or scandalous behaviour. Generally women of honourable families were expected to remain in the private sphere of their own homes to protect not only their own modesty but also their husbands' good reputation. At the same time some women had a significant amount of disposable wealth of their own and were known to have supported rabbis and their ministries; however, they did not participate directly in any of the significant liturgical practices of Judaism. For women of low status, on the other hand, it would not be unusual for them to be seen acting publicly in the marketplace as traders, fisherwomen, bakers or providers of personal services. Some scholars suggest that Mary Magdalene, like many of the other followers of Jesus, was from the lower stratum of society and that her presence in a wandering group of charismatics would therefore not have caused alarm.

In attempting to understand the claim that Mary Magdalene had been healed of seven demons, it is important to know that illness, and particularly mental illness, was thought to be caused by demon possession. The worldview of first century society believed that a struggle between good and evil was taking place and that people could be spirit-possessed by good or evil forces. Many healing practices consequently involved the exorcism of evil spirits that were believed to have entered the body, causing many forms of illness.

Step III: Interpreting the Text

The Women from Galilee

- How many women who were followers of Jesus in Galilee went to Jerusalem with him? Who were most prominent among the women followers? What can we learn about these women, both who they were and what they did? Read: Mark 15:40-41; Matthew 27:55-56; Luke 8:2-3, 23:49; John 19:25.
- The women are described as having been part of Jesus' itinerant ministry, following him from Galilee to Jerusalem. What is involved in being a "follower" of Jesus? Read: Matthew 4:18–22; 10:34–39; 16:24 and Luke 8:1–3, 19–21.
- How do the accounts in Acts 18:24–26 and in Paul's letters (Philippians 4:2–3; Romans 16:1–16) confirm the idea that gospel women were, like their male counterparts, true followers?

Who was Mary Magdalene?

- Both men and women were sometimes named as prostitutes in scripture. Was Mary Magdalene ever named as a prostitute or a sinner? Was "being possessed by demons" necessarily related to sexual sin? Read Luke 8:26-39; 9:37-43; Matthew 15:21-28.
- In what other ways did interpreters try to prove that she was a prostitute? Are these interpretations valid?
- A number of Church Fathers (Hippolytus, Honorius of Autun, St. Ambrose, St. Odo of Cluny, Bernard de Clairvaux and Thomas Aquinas) referred to Mary Magdalene as an "apostle to the apostles." What information from the New Testament texts would lead them to this conclusion? Refer to the chart that was made earlier.
- By what criteria did both Peter and Paul claim the authority of being apostles? Read: Luke 24:34; I Corinthians 15:8–11. Did Mary Magdalene fit the criteria?

The Significance of Mary Magdalene

- All four gospels record Mary Magdalene's presence at the death and resurrection of Jesus. She is the first to experience what the resurrection would mean to his followers. The most insightful account comes from John's gospel (John 20:11–18). What are some of the memorable images of her encounter with Jesus? How do you personally relate to these images? How does John's resurrection story of Mary Magdalene and Jesus compare to Matthew or Luke's versions?

Step IV: Reclaiming the Scriptures for Today

To acquire a better understanding of Mary Magdalene and her role in the ministry of Jesus, scholars also look at primary sources beyond the New Testament.

One such source is the Gnostic writings created in the second half of the first century, at the time when the New Testament gospels were being written. These Gnostic writings reveal another understanding of Mary Magdalene only hinted at in the stories of the New Testament. Although these writings were once widely used, they were considered heretical by the developing orthodox church and not accepted into the canon of the Christian Bible. The Gnostic writings promote the idea that salvation comes through secret knowledge (gnosis) conveyed to its followers from the Risen Christ. The main characters of these writings are the same disciples known from the New Testament - Peter, Thomas, Philip, James and women such as Salome, Mary the mother of Jesus and Mary Magdalene.

In the various books of the Gnostic writings, Mary Magdalene is portrayed as the one who encourages the other disciples to spread the gospel and not to be afraid. The disciples look to her for new revelations that she receives from the Risen Christ. She acquires many titles in the Gnostic writings - Inheritor of the Light, Revealer of Wisdom, the questioner or interlocutrix, and "the apostle who excels the rest." The Gnostic gospel of Philip suggests that Mary Magdalene was very close to Jesus and may have even been his consort.

Mary Magdalene received a great deal of attention during the Middle Ages, and many legends were circulated about her. One such legend written in the thirteenth century describes Mary Magdalene as being attended by angels and fed by them as she is raised two cubits above the earth with her arms extended. Many plays were written about her relationship with Jesus. Artists tended to portray her as a sensuous woman wearing a red dress with long flowing black hair and an alabaster jar near her. Letters and writings of many Church Fathers referred to her as an apostle who was able to undo the failings of Eve and bring eternal life to women. Even a Papal Document in 1868, the Acta Sanctorium, called her an "apostle to the apostles".

- How does this additional information affect your perception of Mary Magdalene?
- What is your assessment of the way Mary Magdalene has been portrayed by both the religious community and the artistic community over the centuries?
- In what ways could Mary Magdalene be reclaimed as a model for women seeking to participate fully in the ministry of the church today?
- A number of people today question whether or not the story of the resurrection of Jesus should be understood as an actual historical event. How might this story, and particularly Mary Magdalene's statement, "I have seen the Lord," be interpreted metaphorically as a message of hope and salvation for Christian people today?

Creative Imagination

- Depict a court hearing that would plead the case that Mary Magdalene was "an apostle to the apostles" and not the "penitent whore" of the Middle Ages.
- Write an entry into Mary Magdalene's diary to portray her thoughts and feelings about her involvement with Jesus' itinerant ministry.
- Donatello created a sculpture of Mary Magdalene in wood (*circa* 1456) that was 188 centimeters high and gilded. He portrayed her as physically worn down yet extremely beautiful. Because he did not offer the usual idealized figure of her, the sculpture compelled viewers to re-examine their perception of Mary Magdalene. Create an artistic representation of Mary Magdalene, as you understand her today using a medium such as fabric, clay, paint or chalk. Portray her as an actual figure or symbolically, using another image to represent her.
- Write a poem to celebrate Mary Magdalene as a role model for women today.
- Other ideas....

Closing Ritual: Women of Strength

Set up a ritual focus in the center of a circle of chairs by using colourful cloths and articles that represent Mary Magdalene, her strength, spirituality and leadership. Have paper and pencils available.

Leader: Ask the participants to share the story of one woman who has been an inspiration to them for the development of their faith. Ask the participants to write the person's name on a piece of paper and place it in a basket that will be passed around the circle.

A Prayer of Thanks for Christian Women:

Pass the basket around the circle again and as each person takes out a name repeat together the following ritual:

We give thanks for...(name of woman) and all that she has meant to us.

Close the ritual by singing Carole Etzler's *Standing Before Us.*

12 Standing Before Us

Carole A. Etzler

2 These are the women who joined
in the struggle
Angry and gentle and wise.
These are the women who called us
to action,
Who called us to open our eyes.

3 These are the women who nurtured
our spirits,
The ones on whom we could depend.
These are the women who gave us
their courage,
Our mentors, our sisters, our friends.

4 These are a few of the women
who led us.
We know there have been many more.
We name but a few, yet we honour
them all,
Those women who went on before.

Martha

She said to him, "Yes Lord, I believe that you are the Messiah, the Son of God, the one coming into the world." *John 11:27*

Scripture Texts: *Luke 10:38–42;*
John 11:1–5, 17–27;
John 12:1–8.

Introduction

Luke's story about two sisters, Mary and Martha, has stimulated considerable controversy through the ages. Martha is portrayed as a busy host, while Mary takes the time to listen to the words of Jesus. In the Middle Ages theologians equated Martha with the active life of ordinary women and Mary with the contemplative pious life. More recently Martha is portrayed as the busy homemaker who has little time for anything else. Women who volunteer for work in the church kitchen or perform social services are often called "Marthas."

It is difficult to understand why Luke chose to write about two sisters who appear to be in competition with each other. Even feminists disagree on the story's usefulness for female role modeling. Is the story meant to suppress women by portraying Mary as listening passively to Jesus, or to encourage them by pointing out that Mary chose more wisely than Martha? Is busy Martha being invited to engage in learning in a similar passive way like Mary? If biblical stories were written to stimulate discussion, this one certainly does!

The story about Martha in John's gospel was most often just simply ignored by church leaders. It is safe to say that John's story was suppressed because it competed with the story of Peter's confession in Matthew 16:15–16. In order to form a balanced portrait of Martha and not label her too quickly, one must read both stories to see her as an individual with a variety of attributes.

Step I: Getting Acquainted with the Text

1. Read each of the texts silently and then ask a participant to read them aloud. How is Martha portrayed in each story?
2. Give your immediate response to that portrayal of Martha.
3. What additional information would you like to have that is not provided in the story?

Step II: Understanding the Text

1. Literary Form

The author of Luke and Acts combines teaching narratives with an orderly historical account of the beginnings of the Christian movement; consequently it is often difficult to separate teaching narratives from historical fact. Many of the stories, such as the one about Martha and Mary, were written as teaching narratives to provide insight into the requirements of true discipleship.

The author of John blends narrative with discourse in which Jesus converses with Martha. This dialogue, much like the parables, creates the feeling of closeness and "personal experience" for the readers. John's distinctive literary style enables him to introduce new concepts of Jesus through the "I am…" statements (John 6:35; 8:12; 11:25).

Both authors use a significant number of stories involving women. While Luke sometimes seems to diminish the role of women in the active ministry of the church, John portrays them as the recipients of major theological insights about Jesus and God.

2. Word Study

to serve: (John 12:2)
Both Luke and John describe Martha as "serving" (John 12:2) or being "distracted by many tasks" (Luke 10:40). The Greek word "*diakonein*" (to serve) has more than one meaning. It can mean "to serve a meal" as any good host would do, but it can also mean to "serve at tables", an important duty in the early Christian community (Acts 6:1–6). The Jesus movement usually gathered for table fellowship, which included a meal followed by a period of teaching and discussion. The task of waiting on tables was important enough to be recognized by the laying on of hands (Acts 6:1–6). Martha may have been serving in this capacity.

the good part: (Luke 10:42)
In the Greek text, Jesus uses the positive form, not the comparative form of "good." It expresses the idea that "only one thing is necessary" for the Jew and that is "to strive for the reign of God" (Luke 12:29–31). Everything else is secondary. Martha is portrayed as being distracted from choosing "the good part." This concern is a common theme in Matthew's as well as in Luke's gospel where Jesus instructs the disciples not to worry or be anxious (Matthew 6:31-34).

Messiah/Christ: (John 11:27)
The Hebrew word *messiah* refers to someone who has been anointed with oil and has been chosen to perform a special task for God. The symbolic act of anointing indicates that the Spirit of God is within that person. In II Samuel 2:4 David was chosen to be the anointed one who would carry out God's plan. In the New Testament the equivalent word for *messiah* is "Christ" which is used to designate Jesus as God's anointed envoy.

The prophetic understanding of the concept of the *messiah* in Hebrew scripture calls for an anointed king who would come from the royal line of David and deliver the Hebrew people (Jeremiah 23:5–6; Micah 5:2; Isaiah 9:6–7). The early Christians believed that Jesus was the fulfillment of this Hebrew prophecy. They upheld Jesus as the "anointed one" empowered by God's spirit to save the Hebrew people and to announce the beginning of the reign of God. There were many different interpretations of just how the deliverance of the Hebrew nation would occur. Some believed that there would be a great holocaust in which the present world would be destroyed and replaced by a new and different one. Others believed that the Messiah would announce a new way to live in the present world, and eventually the reign of God would prevail. The Jews who rejected the Christian idea that Jesus was this long-waited messiah still look for his coming today.

3. Historical Context

By the time both Luke and John were writing their accounts late in the first century, the Christian community had undergone significant change. It was no longer a predominantly Jewish group because converts came from many different ethnic backgrounds, and Gentiles were beginning to outnumber the Jews. John's gospel reflects the anti-Jewish sentiment that grew after a significant break with the synagogue had taken place in the late first century.

The Christian community could no longer depend on the leadership of the original disciples who were being replaced by new leaders and a growing membership that included many women. It became necessary to adopt guidelines for choosing leaders and setting standards for Christian living.

As Christianity spread into the Roman world, the Christian concept of equal participation by all its members came into conflict with the Roman culture that viewed society as a hierarchy of power and position. Rome allowed conquered peoples to manage their own government and worship their own gods, but certain practices of the Christian community were beginning to challenge the Roman way of life. Christians not only encouraged celibacy for both men and women, it also allowed slaves to be equal members within the Christian community. Romans judged such activities to be a threat to the household code that governed their lives. When Christians professed that Christ was the one and only saviour of the world, the superiority of Rome's own religion was threatened. By the time Luke and John did their writing, concessions were already being made by Christians to accommodate Roman ways in order to avoid discrimination and persecution. It became increasingly dangerous to be a Christian. Luke and John responded to this situation in their gospels by explaining that Jesus was the Messiah and by encouraging their communities to remain faithful.

Step III: Interpreting the Text

Getting to know Martha

- Begin to build a portrait of Martha from the two texts. How would you describe her to someone who has never heard about her? What qualities does she possess? What details from the story are missing?
- How does the portrayal of Martha by John differ from that of Luke? How is it similar?
- What does the messianic statement in John tell us about Martha's faith?
- What important divine revelation did Jesus share with Martha? What other woman in John's gospel had a similar experience with Jesus (John 4:1–42)?
- What was John's purpose for telling the story of Martha?

A famous medieval legend from the south of France describes how Martha was able to tame a dragon (the symbol of evil and of the old order) by using a cross and holy water. She was also famous for her healing and teaching abilities. Pictures and stained glass windows have kept alive these traditional stories.

- Why do you think these legends about Martha became so popular?

Step IV: Reclaiming the Scriptures for Today

- In John's gospel Martha confesses that Jesus is the Christ. It parallels the confession by Peter in the other gospels (Matthew 16:15–16). Give reasons to explain why it is important for women and men today to be aware of her confession and of the context in which it was given. What might John be trying to say about women who would like to share in the ministry of the church?
- How did Jesus' understanding of resurrection differ from Martha's? What are the implications of Jesus' understanding of resurrection for the foundation of faith today? What does it mean to free ourselves from the limits imposed by death and suffering in order to be able to engage in the new life possibilities promised by Jesus?
- The legacy of Jesus and who he really was is sometimes labeled as "a dangerous memory." Using the two stories about Martha, give reasons why some people make this assessment of Jesus and his work?
- The legend of Martha taming the dragon symbolizes the struggle against evil. How do women and men work against such forces in today's world? Name some of the organizations that seek to make the world a better place for everyone. Describe how they do this.
- How does Martha's story in Luke and John address some of the issues that confront the church today, such as who can interpret scripture and who can represent God and Jesus?

Creative Imagination

- Write a legend about Martha to show how she would struggle against evil in today's world.
- Make a collage using symbols that represent the importance of Martha as a disciple.
- Rewrite the story of Martha and Mary from Luke's gospel filling in the missing details to show what might have been taking place during Jesus' visit.
- Write a poem or hymn in praise of Martha for the strength of her faith.
- Other ideas....

Closing Ritual: "Who do YOU say I am?"

Have participants bring a picture of Jesus that captures their understanding of who he is. Place the pictures on the ritual table in the center of the circle.

Sing a few of your favourite songs about Jesus (a verse or two of each song).

Read together John 11:27, Martha's confession of Jesus as the Christ.

Ask participants to share what Jesus means to them for their journey in the Christian faith.

In closing say together:

Open our minds to hear once again the words of Jesus;
Who he was,
What he did,
How he offered a new way to live.
Like Martha, may we also understand Jesus' message
For the world! Amen

The Woman At The Well

Then the woman left her water jar and went back to the city. John 4:28

Scripture Texts: John 4:1-42.

Introduction

The story of the Woman at the Well is perhaps one of the most important narratives in the New Testament because it contains a profound discussion about the nature of God and about Jesus as the Messiah.

This narrative is typical of a number of biblical stories in which an unnamed woman plays a major role. An ancient legend recorded in the Roman Martyrology gives the Samaritan woman at the well the name "Photina," a latinized version of the Greek form "Photeine," an adjective meaning radiant light which is derived from the noun "phos"(light). The legend relates how Photina preached the gospel in many places, and after being imprisoned in Carthage, was martyred for her faith. The legend of Photina was always more popular in the East among Greek Orthodox women than in the West. In the Greek Orthodox calendar Photina is commemorated on the fifth Sunday of Easter for her missionary work in spreading the gospel.

The Samaritan woman was once highly regarded by church leaders such as Augustine, John Chrysostom and Origen as a disciple and apostle who led others to Christ. Hymn writers as well as the leaders of the Eastern Orthodox Church celebrated her contribution. In later years, however, her role in the formation of the early church was diminished when interpreters began to portray her as an immoral woman needing the forgiveness of Christ.

Step I: Getting Acquainted with the Text

1. Read the text silently and then ask a participant to read it aloud. Pay particular attention to the theological discussion between the Samaritan

woman and Jesus.

2. Give your immediate response to the portrayal of the Samaritan woman and her role in the story.
3. Jot down any questions you have about the story.

Step II: Understanding the Text

1. Literary Form

Biblical scholars designate this story as an "instruction" narrative. The author of John's gospel takes the reader on a journey to discover the true identity of Jesus and the nature of God. The readers are invited to enter into the story by identifying with the woman at the well as she gradually uncovers the identity of Jesus. The author's use of a question-and-answer dialogue is a teaching technique used frequently in the gospels. The lively exchange between the woman and Jesus creates suspense and heightens the reader's interest. The story is rich in symbolism that reinterprets ancient Hebrew motifs for Christian use.

2. Word Study

Samaritans: (John 4:9)
The Hebrew people of Judah in the south and Israel in the north had originally shared a common heritage and were at one time politically unified under David's kingdom. The reference to Jacob's well where Jesus met the Samaritan woman points to this common heritage. When the Assyrians defeated Israel in 722 BCE, they completely destroyed the government of Israel, and most of the population was deported to Media and Persia. The Assyrians then permitted immigrants from other countries such as Babylon and Cuthah to settle the area around Samaria (II Kings 17:24). These immigrants along with the Israelites who had not been deported were known as Samaritans.

At first the immigrants brought their own gods to Samaria, but later they converted to the worship of the Hebrew God (II Kings 17:25-34). Antipathy developed between the Jews of the south and the Samaritans, because the Samaritans continued to worship their own gods as well as Yahweh. The Jews from the south believed the northern tribes of Israelites had been destroyed because they disobeyed the ancient laws and disregarded the prophets who warned them that Assyria would defeat them (II Kings 17:13-20). Animosity between the two nations was often expressed in violent attacks on each other.

The Israelites in the south claimed that the Samaritans were not "pure" Jews because most of the original population had been dispersed and replaced by people from other countries.

When the Hebrews rebuilt the Temple in Jerusalem after their return from exile in Babylon, the Samaritans were not permitted to assist in the reconstruction. As a consequence of this rejection, the Samaritans tried to prevent the Temple's completion (Ezra 4:1-10) and later opposed the rebuilding of the walls of Jerusalem (Nehemiah 4:1-23).

on this mountain: (John 4:20)
In the wilderness, after the Exodus from Egypt, God made a covenant with the Hebrew people at Mount Sinai. When the Hebrews crossed the Jordan and entered the Promised Land, they renewed their covenant with God on Mount Gerizim (Deuteronomy 11:29). That mountain became the dwelling place of God for the Samaritans (John 4:20). Later the Hebrew people in Judah built the Temple at Mount Zion in Jerusalem and claimed that this was the dwelling place of God (I Kings 6:11-13). Disputes then arose between the Israelites and the Samaritans, each claiming they possessed the true place of worship.

Jacob's well: (John 4:6)
The location of the story at Jacob's well reminds the readers that both the Samaritans and the Israelites can trace their roots to the patriarch who dug the well (John 4:5-6,12; Genesis 33:18-20). This common connection emphasizes the Samaritans' right to receive the new revelation brought by Jesus.

The association of God with water as a life-giving force and with the well as a place to find salvation has a long history in the Jewish tradition and is expressed many times in Hebrew scripture (John 4:13-14; Isaiah 12:2-3). By placing Jesus beside the ancient well, the author links him to an earlier prophetic understanding of God.

3. Historical Context

By 90 CE the Christian community included a great variety of ethnic and social groups. It is very likely, therefore, that Jews, Samaritans, Gnostics and Gentiles were the recipients of John's gospel. Perhaps the story of the Samaritan woman was written to approve of the diversity of believers within the Jesus movement.

To appreciate the full significance of this story it is necessary to understand the implications of the deep animosity that exited between the Jews and the Samaritans. Over the years there were many skirmishes and border attacks initiated by both groups. Jesus' decision to travel through Samaria presented a bold challenge to this situation of mutual animosity. By speaking publicly to a woman and accepting water from her, Jesus also violated several fundamental social taboos. His unconventional actions give rise to a story that has as its central character a woman who not only hears the words of Jesus, but acts upon them.

Step III: Interpreting the Text

Over the years various interpretations of the Samaritan woman have seriously maligned her character, depicting her as sinful. Some opinions expressed about her include:

- She had five husbands because each of them had divorced her.
- She was living in sin because the man she was living with was not her husband. She was, therefore, assumed to be a prostitute or a sexually promiscuous woman (John 4:18).
- She came to the well late and alone (it was noon) because she was ashamed to be noticed by the other women.
- She began asking Jesus questions to distract him from criticizing her immorality.
- The villagers had to come to see Jesus for themselves because she was not a credible witness (John 4:39-42).
- She could not have been an apostle because, being a woman, she wasn't capable of understanding the substance of Jesus' ideas.

Is there any evidence to support these interpretations about her character and capabilities? Where might interpreters get these ideas? Suggest alternative explanations for her behaviour and actions.

Getting to know the Samaritan woman, later known as Photina

- How would you describe Photina? How old might she have been? What kind of person was she?
- What further details would you like to know about her? What questions are not answered about her marital status?
- Why do you think Jesus asked her to go "call your husband and come

back" (John 4:16)? Why did Jesus accept her response?

- Why do you think Jesus chose to reveal to her so much about himself and about God?
- Why is she sometimes called the first missionary of the Christian faith?

The Theological Discussion

- How many times is the word "truth" in its different variations used in this text? What is the significance of these references to truth?
- Discuss the theological issues raised in these texts: John 4:7-15; John 4:19-24; John 4:25-26 and 42.
- Why would this understanding of God be "good news" to a Samaritan woman and her neighbours?
- In what ways has this study changed your opinion of the woman at the well? Explain why.

Step IV: Reclaiming the Scriptures for Today

- If this is a narrative designed to draw the audience into the story how successfully were you drawn in? How do you relate to the woman at the well?
- How might this story inspire a woman to seek ordination in the church today?
- This story was probably seen as a scandalous story when it was first read (John 4:9, 27). Is it still a scandalous story today? Give reasons for your answer.
- In what ways were the social norms of the day being challenged by Jesus when he spoke to the woman at the well? What social norms need to be challenged in our society?
- How might this story be used to preach against racism and religious intolerance? How might it be used in the struggle for women's equality in church and society?
- What concept of God is revealed in Jesus' conversation with Photina? In what other ways would you name or image God?

Creative Imagination

- Elaborate on Photina's thoughts about Jesus, who, after all, was a foreigner in her country. Write an entry into Photina's diary.
- Write a legal defense for the courts of the church on behalf of Photina's right to be called a disciple and an apostle.

- Write a poem about Photina's jar and the significance of the act of leaving it behind (John 4:28).
- Plan a feast day for Photina. What might be your focus? What activities would you include? What food might you share?
- Other ideas....

Closing Ritual: The Nature of God

Create a ritual focus by placing a cloth on a table that is located in the center of a circle. Place a large bowl of water on the table with small "tea light" candles around the bowl (enough for each person). Provide matches.

Sing or read the words of Brian Wren's hymn *Bring Many Names* (*Voices United*, page 268).

Ask the participants to share their thoughts about the image or nature of God that is most meaningful to them. When they share their reflections have each participant light a candle and place it in the bowl of water.

Close the ritual by asking the participants to call out the great diversity of names and images for God.

Prisca (also known as Priscilla)

Apollos began to speak boldly in the synagogue; but when Priscilla and Aquila heard him, they took him aside and explained the Way of God to him more accurately. *Acts 18:26*

Scripture Texts: *Acts 18:1-3, 18-19, 24-28;*
Romans 16:3-5;
I Corinthians 16:19;
II Timothy 4:19.

Introduction

Women began as equals within the charismatic Christian community. Prisca's story is one small part of a larger account of women's involvement in the church's early development. Her story, along with references to other women in Acts and Paul's letters, affirms the notion that the early Christian church functioned as an egalitarian community. Although the biblical references to women's roles in the early church are sparse and scattered, when drawn together they create a picture of women taking part in every aspect of the Christian community—teaching, preaching, healing, prophesying, and evangelizing.

Luke records in Acts 1 and 2 that women as well as men were present at the time of Pentecost when "all together" they were filled with the gift of the Holy Spirit. Paul's letters reveal that a number of women were his co-workers who were responsible for the formation of house churches throughout the Mediterranean.

The equal participation of women in the Christian community was, however, short lived. In the early years women's participation went unchallenged because the church functioned in the private sphere of the home. The Greco-Roman culture that the church encountered as it expanded and grew in numbers required men and women to adhere to strict gender roles. Men were expected to function in the public sphere, while women were confined to the private. As the church developed its own hierarchy women found participation in a public ministry much more difficult.

Step I: Getting Acquainted with the Text

1. Read the texts silently, and then ask a participant to read each one aloud.
2. Give your immediate response to the texts.
3. Make a list of questions that arise concerning the role of women in the early church.

Step II: Understanding the Text

1. Literary Form

References to Prisca and to her work come from two different sources in scripture. In his history of the early church, Luke records Prisca's encounter with Apollos as part of the missionary work of spreading the gospel. Paul confirms Prisca's role, calling her a co-worker. While the historical accuracy of Luke's account may be questioned because it was written some time after the events, Paul's references to her come from letters that were actually sent to the churches. Paul's relationship to Prisca is described in Romans 16:3 and I Corinthians 16:19.

- What is the significance of the fact that Prisca is mentioned in more than one letter? (Romans 16, I Corinthians 16 and II Timothy 4:19).

2. Word Study

Prisca/Priscilla:
In Acts, Luke uses the name Priscilla which is a diminutive of Prisca, the name used by Paul. She is always partnered with her husband Aquila in a team ministry. In the four of the six times she is named in the New Testament her name appears before her husband's name. Scholars conclude from this naming order that Prisca was more prominent than her husband in giving leadership in the church.

work with me in Christ Jesus: (Romans 16:3)
When the Greek word *ergon* (work) is used in a Christian context, it refers to the work that is done "for the Lord" (I Corinthians 3:9). Paul frequently uses this term to describe his co-workers who are both men and women. In Romans

16 he commends several women who have "worked hard in the Lord"—Prisca, Mary, Junia, Tryphaena, Tryphosa and Persis. Paul also names men such as Timothy (I Thessalonians 3:2), Titus (II Corinthians 8:23) and others (Philemon 1:24) as fellow workers.

the church in their house: (Romans 16:5)
The house church was the original meeting place for the early Christian community. Both women and men are recorded as providing their homes for religious meetings (I Corinthians 16:19; Philemon 1:1-2; Colossians 4:15). Believers from all levels of society met on the first day of the week to share a common meal, to listen to an itinerant preacher (often an apostle), and to engage in discussion (Acts 20:7-11). Believers included Jews, Gentiles, men, women, children, slaves, and former slaves (Galatians 3:28). Although some people of wealth participated in the early Christian community, the majority of believers came from lower economic and social classes. Members performed a variety of roles within the group, but there was no hierarchy of officers. According to scripture, participants spoke and acted through the power of the Holy Spirit within them.

Once the followers of Jesus were committed to spreading the good news of his life and resurrection, many house churches were formed to carry out this mission. These churches began mainly in urban centers and gradually spread throughout the Mediterranean area to cities such as Antioch, Damascus, Ephesus, Corinth, Rome, Thessalonica, Cenchreae and Philippi. In some cases there was more than one house church in a city.

- Locate these cities on a biblical map of the Middle East.

3. Historical Context

The Christian church spread rapidly, but it was not a cohesive community. There were many diverse beliefs and practices with no central authority in control except for the teachings of the apostles. Members saw themselves as living their lives "in the Spirit," which was a free and open expression of their faith. Consequently, there was a constant need to clarify and explain the meaning of Jesus as the Messiah and what it meant to live "in the Spirit." Both Paul and Prisca, as well as others, were involved in explaining and encouraging membership in the Way of God.

- What made it possible for so many people of different social and religious backgrounds to come together as an egalitarian community (I Corinthians 12:12-13; Galatians 3:23-29)?

- What problems might have caused dissension within the community because of this diversity (I Corinthians 7:17-24; 11:18-22)?

Step III: Interpreting the Text

Getting to know Prisca (Acts 18)

- Where did Paul meet Prisca and her husband Aquila?
- Why were Prisca and Aquila not in Rome?
- What was the relationship between Prisca and Paul (Acts 18:2-3,18-19; Romans 16:3-5)?
- Where did Prisca and Aquila start a house church? Did they do this before or after meeting Paul?

Prisca as teacher

- Who was Apollos (Acts 18:24-28)?
- What was the "Way of God" that Prisca and Aquila needed to "explain to Apollos more accurately" (Luke 3:15-16; Acts 1:4-5; 2:1-4)?
- What is the significance of the fact that Prisca could teach such a person as Apollos and not be criticized (Acts 18:24-25)?
- How did Paul feel about Prisca's work in the church (Romans 16:3-4; I Corinthians 16:19)?

Step IV: Reclaiming the Scriptures for Today

- List the evidence that supports the idea that many women like Prisca were involved in the ministry of the early church? (Romans 16, especially v7; Acts 2:14-21; 17:1-4; 22:2-5; Galatians 3:28; Philippians 4:2-3).
- How does the account of Prisca's activities give authority for women in ministry today? How does her story contradict Paul's instructions to women in his letter to the Corinthians (I Corinthians 11:1-16) as well as the restrictions placed on women by the author of I Timothy (I Timothy 2:11-15)? Why do you think Paul and the author of Timothy are advocating restrictions on women's participation?
- Do women today need the authority of scripture to justify their desire to have equal participation with men in the ministry of the church? Give reasons for your answer.

- Judging from the structure and practices of your own denominational church, how has the present day church changed from the early church? How do you feel about these changes?
- How has the charismatic nature of the early church been diminished by the growth of the institutional church? Today many people describe the presence of the divine as spirituality. What does this term mean to you? How do modern Christians express spirituality as part of their faith?

Creative Imagination

- Imagine the gathering of a first-century house church and write a plan for such a gathering. What activities would be involved? Who would lead it? Who would attend it? What topic might be discussed?
- Phoebe (Romans 16:1-2) and Prisca were both friends of Paul, and all three were involved in similar missionary work. Write an imaginary letter from Prisca to Phoebe. What might they say to each other about their work, about Paul and about their hopes for the future?
- Design a table runner to honour the women workers of the early Christian community. Choose a symbol to represent each woman. Use appliqué, embroidery or fabric markers to put these ideas on the cloth.
- Other ideas....

Closing Ritual: In the Spirit of Pentecost

Set up four large candles on the meditation center (provide matches). Ask four people from the circle group to light each candle as they give thanks for the Spirit that lives among us.

Candle #1: We give thanks for the comforting Spirit that comes to us in our time of need, when we are anxious about many things, when we feel oppressed and undervalued. (Pause for meditation.)

Candle #2: We give thanks for the Spirit that challenges us to find new and better ways to relate to one another; for the Spirit that calls us to take risks in the struggle for justice. (Pause for meditation.)

Candle #3: We give thanks for the Spirit that sustains us when we need strength and clarity of purpose, when we need to persist with patience. (Pause for meditation.)

Candle #4: We give thanks for the Spirit that calls us to open our eyes to discrimination, to inequality, to see when others are hurting and changes are needed. (Pause for meditation.)

Sing Carolyn McDade's *Spirit of Life* (*Voices United,* page 381) or another song of the Spirit from your own faith tradition.

Share an experience when the Spirit was at work in your life either personally or in a community.

Close the ritual by saying together:

Spirit of Life,
Within and without,
Make your presence known to us.
Call us to the awareness that leads to action.
Celebrate with us a new way to live.
Amen

Introduction to the Monologues

The quilted portrayals of five biblical women have been presented across Ontario many times during the past eight years. The title of the presentation, *Some Women Amazed Us*, was inspired by a short verse from Luke 24:22. The combination of the visual (quilts) with the spoken word (monologues) proved to be an inviting way to present new and challenging insights into the biblical women's stories.

Eve: The Mother of All Living

Huldah

Mary Magdalene

The Woman at the Well

Martha

"Some Women Amazed Us"

Archeological digs, fragments of ancient texts and women's curiosity about their own heritage have inspired a number of women to seek a new interpretation of the biblical stories which portray the lives of women.

Unfortunately, until recently, it was only men who interpreted scripture. In the past, male scholars have chosen to interpret scripture in ways that depict women as inferior to men, as sinners who are sexually promiscuous and, therefore, not as worthy as men to be God's representatives.

When I began my search into scripture a few years ago, I found very little evidence to support this kind of interpretation, and I came to the conclusion that traditions and folklore outside scripture had been imposed on the biblical stories, and it was these overlays that contributed so much to the negative portrayal of women.

There is an urgent need to have a fresh look at scripture. We must understand that these negative portrayals of women have caused serious harm to women and their self-image, as well as to women's relationships with men. We must realize how deeply these beliefs from the past still affect our lives today.

The women of the Bible have been unfairly treated. In my research, contrary to general opinion, I found the women to be strong and courageous, eager to find answers to important theological questions, willing to take risks and above all, devoted disciples. Moved by this new insight, I wanted to share with others what I had discovered. I chose the medium of quilting to do this.

I know that not everyone will agree with my interpretations, or what I have chosen to emphasize. There are many ways to interpret these stories, but I have based my presentation on the sound scholarship of both male and female theologians. These quilts are the result of my own intense need to find answers to questions that have bothered me for some time. I want to portray these women in an honest and credible way. And so I bring the stories of these five women to you in the form of monologues.

Eve: The Mother of All Living

My name is Eve. Throughout history I have been portrayed as a sexual seductress, a sinful woman, the cause of evil in the world. I have been accused of bringing about the downfall of humanity, the reason why you are not now living in the Garden of Eden.

But look at me! I am a pregnant woman. Many people forget that Adam called me Eve because I am "The Mother of All Living". After we ate the fruit, Adam and I became aware of our creative powers. We became partners with God. When we left the garden to go into the world, exciting new challenges and opportunities awaited us.

My story is a story about the celebration of life, not one of death and punishment. Nowhere in the Hebrew text does it say that I enticed, seduced or tricked Adam into eating the fruit. It merely says, "she gave some to her husband, who was with her, and he ate". In fact, I had not yet been created when God gave Adam the direct command not to eat the fruit. In his letter to the Romans, the apostle Paul speaks only of Adam's transgression, not mine. Somewhere along the way I became the scapegoat for every evil act. Tertullian, a Church Father from the second century, when addressing women wrote these words: "Do you not know that you are each an Eve. You are the devil's gateway. On account of you even the Son of God had to die."

I took the fruit out of curiosity. The fruit looked good to eat and the serpent said it would make me wise. I had no evil intent. I did not yet know the difference between right and wrong, good and evil. It was only after I ate the fruit that I gained the knowledge of choice and its consequences.

My story, at the beginning of scripture, is just part of a larger tale. It teaches us that God will not abandon humanity despite its shortcomings, weaknesses and all its foolish mistakes. It is really the story of the partnership of humankind and the divine.

In my wall hanging the fabric and symbols were chosen to express the celebration of life. I am pregnant and my name is "Eve, the Mother of All Living". So that you will not forget what has been said about me, I am surrounded by the symbols that have been used to malign my character–the forbidden fruit and the serpent.

The side panels display a mixture of beautiful flowers, wheat and fruit emphasizing the abundance and joy of creation. Below and above is a panel of quilted *yonis*–an ancient female fertility symbol. In each corner is another ancient symbol found in many parts of the world; it has been named the "birthing symbol". It images a woman's body, her arms and her legs, and a baby in her womb.

The apple design in the top and bottom panels is a curious mixture of blossom and mature fruit–an excellent symbol for God as the Alpha and the Omega, the beginning and the end. The apple symbol illustrates the assurance of God's promise not to abandon us but to be constantly present among us.

Huldah

My story is typical of the "forgotten women" of the Bible, yet the part I played was crucial to the survival of the Hebrew nation. The account of what I did was recorded in two books of the Bible, II Kings, and a later history called Chronicles. A similar report can be found in a history of the Jews entitled *Antiquities*. It was written by Josephus, a first century Jewish historian. Please note that my story was important enough to be recorded several times.

What is my story? It occurred during the reign of King Josiah. An ancient document was found when renovations were being made in the Temple. Because it looked important, it was taken to the king who sensed immediately that it required interpretation. So he decided to send his top five officials, all men, to the court prophet to inquire of the Lord the meaning of this document.

The prophet they consulted was *me*, Huldah. I gave my prophecy in the form used by all the prophets before me. I began by saying, "Thus says the Lord". I warned King Josiah that Judah was to be destroyed because his people had not been living according to God's way. Obviously, I spoke with authority because he followed my advice. He began to purify the Hebrew religion, got rid of pagan practices and reinstated ancient Hebrew rites.

I lived in the Second Quarter next to the Temple complex, and I was part of the educated élite of the religious establishment. My use of the well-known phrase, "Thus says the Lord" placed me in the long prophetic tradition that embraced prophets such as Isaiah and my contemporary, Jeremiah. In those days it was not easy to fulfill the requirements of a true prophet. The standard was Moses. But I was able to live up to that standard and I was held in high regard.

In my wall hanging the Hebrew words above and below reflect the essence of my prophecy. Taken from Deuteronomy it says, " I [God] set before you this day a blessing and a curse." The Jewish religion teaches that humans are able to make choices, but they must also accept responsibility for the resulting consequences.

The dark panel above represents the curse and the grape vines below, the eucharistic blessing.

Behind me is a representation of the wall of Jerusalem where you will find a pair of gates. These were once known as Huldah's Gates, named in my honour.

The Star of David and the menorah candles in each corner represent the present state of Israel. My prophecy assured the survival of the Hebrew nation. You might say that I was a saviour figure. I warned the king that not even he was above the Torah—the law. It is the responsibility of all people, rich or poor, to follow God's way of love and justice.

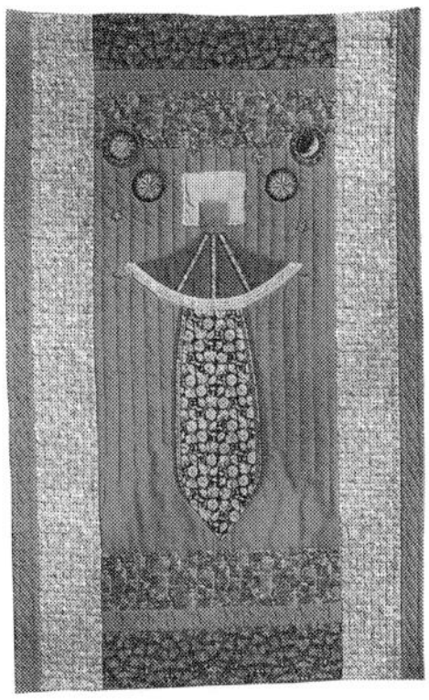

Mary Magdalene

I am another woman who has been much maligned and misrepresented. My name is Mary Magdalene. During the early centuries of the church and into the Middle Ages people interpreted who I was and what I did in two very different ways.

One idea that became extremely popular was the teaching that I was a terrible sinner, and a prostitute whose horrendous sin was forgiven by Christ and replaced with ultimate grace. During the Middle Ages church leaders upheld me as a model for all women, because they considered all women to be the sinful daughters of Eve. I was given the name "penitent whore". How did I acquire such an awful title?

In Luke's gospel I am named as one of Jesus' followers. A few verses before there is a story about a woman, a sinner from the city, who washed Jesus' feet with her tears and her hair. Although there is no biblical evidence that I was this sinner, early Church Fathers encouraged the idea that we were one and the same person.

Defenders of this interpretation point to the fact that I was healed of seven demons. And that these demons were the cause of my sexual immorality. It is interesting to note, however, that when other people in scripture were healed of demons, they were never accused of sexual immorality. Actually my problem was connected to mental anguish and anxiety—a common ailment in those days. I should have been given a badge of honour for having received such a dramatic healing. Instead it was used to condemn me.

Some interpreters of my story point to the fact that I came from Magdala, which had a bad reputation as a port city where many prostitutes lived. They concluded that I must have been one of them.

A number of Church Fathers portrayed me as a composite woman, making me all the unnamed women of the gospels. Some claimed that I was not only the sinner from the city, but also the adulteress brought before Jesus, and even the woman at the well.

But some Church Fathers, such as Bernard de Clairvaux and Thomas Aquinas, saw me in another way. They gave me the title "Apostle to the Apostles". They called me this because I had witnessed the crucifixion and resurrection of Jesus, and Jesus himself had commissioned me to tell the others what I had seen and heard. The *Gnostic Gospels*, Christian writings not included in the Bible, also tell how I had visions of the Risen Christ in which he continued to reveal his special knowledge. I interpreted these teachings to the disciples, and they began to call me the "questioner".

In my wall hanging I am portrayed in the shape of a cross because of my intimate and profound connection to the crucifixion and resurrection of Jesus. I am wearing rich ecclesiastical garments—purple and gold. Because of all that I did, I have often wondered if I should have been the first pope, or at the very least have stood beside Peter at the beginning of the apostolic succession.

One would have to admit that had I applied for this position, my credentials would have been flawless. Just listen:

- As a teacher I had first hand knowledge of Jesus' teachings because I was part of his itinerant ministry.
- I was a patron who financially supported his ministry.
- I put my life at risk to be at the crucifixion.
- I remained loyal to him, ministering to him in his time of need, and I was not among those who fled.
- I was the first to experience his resurrection as recorded in all four gospels.
- I was certainly an apostle, commissioned by Christ himself to tell the others.

In the wall hanging two towers of stone surround me. My name *Magdalene* comes from a Hebrew word which means tower or stronghold. In a letter, written in 412, St. Jerome referred to me as the one who was "called the tower because of the earnestness and the glow of her faith". This word *Magdalene* was like a title that had been given to me.

The alabaster jars in the panels above and below stress the connection that was made between me and the gospel women who anointed Jesus. Portraits of me from the Middle Ages usually include this symbol of the alabaster jar.

The stars have seven main points to remind you that I was healed of a significant ailment, my badge of honour as a healed person.

I have a square halo. In a Roman basilica there is an ancient mosaic portraying female figures. Three of them have round halos because they had already died when the mosaic was made. One of them has a square halo because at the time she was still alive. I have a square halo because I want you to see me as still very, very much alive. I am an excellent model for the modern church woman.

The Woman at the Well

When Jesus was passing through Samaria, he stopped at Jacob's well. When I came to draw water he asked me, a Samaritan woman, for a drink. He took this opportunity to start a conversation about spiritual matters. He used the metaphor of real water to talk about the living water of eternal life. I eagerly asked for this special water because I thought it could end the drudgery of having to draw water everyday. Jesus thought that I did not understand, but he saw that I was curious and interested, so for some reason, he asked me to go and get my husband. When I told him that I had no husband he pointed out that I was right, that I had had five husbands and was now living with someone who was not my husband.

From this conversation, interpreters of my story have assumed that I had had five husbands because I had been sexually promiscuous. They inferred that I must have been divorced, unable to keep a husband and was therefore living in sin. Such an interpretation is not the only way to understand my situation. My husbands could have died, from illness, accident or war. Scripture does not give the details. There was a marriage practice in ancient Israel called *levirate marriage*. If a woman's husband died one of his brothers could take her as his wife to keep the family and property intact. Sometimes the last brother was not able to marry her, but he might still take her into his household. This could have been my situation. I could have suffered a life of sorrow and hardship. Your biblical story does not provide the details of my situation.

Other suggestions have been made over the years to confirm my status as a prostitute. It has been suggested that I came late to the well—it was noon—to avoid the other women because of my shame. Some even inferred that I came late because I had been working as a prostitute all night!

Jesus did not condemn me in any way. He seemed more impressed that I did not hide the truth.

When I realized that he was a learned man, a prophet, I engaged him in a serious theological question. Historically the Jews and Samaritans began as a common people, worshipping the same God. But because of wars, deportations and intermarriage, the Samaritans were no longer considered by the Jews in the south to be what might be called "pure Jews". Both, however, continued to claim God as their own. This of course led to a long and bitter conflict between them. I wanted to know where God really dwelt—on my mountain in Samaria or in his Temple in Jerusalem. Jesus replied that neither was the truth. God is Spirit and can be worshipped anywhere.

When I told him that a Messiah was to come to reveal all things he chose me to disclose that he was the one who was to come.

I was so excited I ran off to the village to tell the others the good news—that the messiah had come and was sitting beside Jacob's well. In my excitement I left my jar behind just like the disciples who left their fishing nets behind. The villagers believed my story and left the village to see for themselves. I had credibility among my neighbours!

In the wall hanging I have five coins on my headdress honouring my five husbands. In the panel above, doves represent the free spirit of God that is available to all. This panel will remind you that I had an important theological discussion with Jesus there at the well.

There was so much excitement that day that even the dry, brown earth was dancing!

The Greek Orthodox Church has given me a name, Photina, which means "shining light". Every year they celebrate a feast day honouring me as the first missionary who took the Good News beyond the Jewish people.

Martha

Most of you know me as a diligent homemaker, but in this wall hanging I am dealing with a dragon. I am Martha. This is not a biblical idea of course, but rather a legend from the Middle Ages. Many legends grew up around myself, my brother Lazarus and Mary Magdalene—how we fled from Palestine after the death of Jesus because our lives were in danger. It is said that we set out across the Mediterranean and landed in southern France where we continued to teach and to heal. Stories spread about our miraculous healing powers. Among them was this story about me. St. George killed the dragon, but I was said to have tamed it with the help of the cross and holy water. This legend has been preserved in stain glass windows and paintings in southern France.

My biblical story is found in Luke's gospel. I appear to have been reprimanded for working too hard at domestic duties while Mary, my sister, is praised for sitting at the feet of Jesus, learning from him. This has always been a difficult story to understand. It seems to set the two of us in competition with each other and to contradict the basic Jewish teaching of service to others and the important custom of hospitality.

There was controversy over the interpretation of this story even in the Middle Ages. Some Church Fathers used me as an example of the active life of ordinary women, while Mary symbolized the contemplative, prayerful life which received a great deal of praise.

Perhaps Luke told the story this way to emphasize the need to seek first the reign of God before anything else and to see this pursuit as the most important thing one can do. Several times throughout the whole gospel narrative Jesus expressed this idea to all the disciples, not just to me.

John's gospel contains another story about me, but it is labeled as "The Raising of Lazarus", so the part I played often gets little attention. Here, as in Luke's gospel, I am portrayed as a strong-willed person who speaks up for herself. When Jesus does not return to heal Lazarus and he dies, I was blunt with Jesus and I said, " If you had been here, my brother would not have died."

In spite of this reprimand Jesus knew that I still trusted him, so he chose that moment to reveal to me that he was the resurrection and the life and my brother would not die. I responded to him by saying, " I believe that you are the Messiah, the Son of God, the one coming into the world." Although my statement of belief parallels that of Peter's confession that is recorded in the other gospels, it has never received the same attention. Instead, the focus has been shifted to concentrate on the raising of Lazarus.

In my wall hanging the Medieval legend captures the impression of me as a woman of strength and conviction—one who can put down the forces of evil as symbolized by the dragon.

My apron should remind you of my diaconal role of service and hospitality, an important part of the table fellowship of the early church.

The crosses symbolize my belief in Jesus as the Messiah. He chose me, a woman, to reveal himself as the resurrection and the life and I understood what he meant.

My story has been kept alive by the legends, paintings, stained glass windows and churches built in my honour.

I am a model worthy of your emulation and respect.

Conclusion

The stories of these five women are like hidden treasures that have been found once again-pearls of great price! In their various roles, the women provide us with models that are exciting, courageous, intelligent and life-giving. Like Eve, and her husband Adam, we need to celebrate our capacity to be co-creators in partnership with God. Like Huldah, we must stand firm in our demand for justice. As teachers and learners, we must ask difficult questions just like Mary Magdalene and Photina were willing to do. And finally, like Martha, we must stand and be counted and be willing to confront the evils of this world if there is to be a good and abundant life for all!

Women should be able to hear these stories as sources of inspiration that can sustain and nurture their faith. These stories clearly show that women have a noble and worthy heritage that supports their desire to share in the ministry of God's work.

BIBLIOGRAPHY

Barnavi, Eli, Ed. *A Historical Atlas of the Jewish People*. New York: Alfred A. Knopf, 1992.

Bauckham, Richard. *Gospel Women*. Grand Rapids: Wm. B. Eerdmans, 2002.

Bellis, Alice Ogden. *Helpmates, Harlots, and Heroes*. Louisville: Westminster/ John Knox, 1994.

Boulding, Elise. *The Underside of History*. Boulder, Colorado: Westview Press, 1976.

Brown, Raymond. *The Community of the Beloved Disciple*. New York: Paulist Press, 1979.

Brown, Robert McAfee. *Unexpected News*. Philadelphia: The Westminster Press, 1984.

Brown, Raymond, K. Donfried, J. Fitzmyer and J. Reumann, Eds. *Mary in the New Testament*. New York: Paulist Press, 1978.

Campbell, Edward F. Jr. *Ruth*. Garden City: Doubleday, 1975.

Crossan, John Dominic. *The Birth of Christianity*. New York: HarperCollins, 1998.

Crossan, J. D. and J. L. Reed. *Excavating Jesus*. New York: HarperCollins, 2001.

Day, Peggy L. Ed. *Gender and Difference in Ancient Israel*. Minneapolis: Fortress Press, 1989.

Diamant, Anita. *The Red Tent*. New York: Picador USA, 1997.

Fiorenza, Elizabeth Schüssler. *In Memory of Her: A Feminist Theological Reconstruction of Christian Origins*. New York: Crossroad, 1985.

________. *But She Said*. Boston: Beacon Press, 1992.

Frymer-Kensky, Tikva. *In the Wake of the Goddesses*. New York: The Free Press, 1992.

____________. *Reading the Women of the Bible*. New York: Schocken Books, 2002.

Gebara, I. and M. C. Bingemer. *Mary, Mother of God, Mother of the Poor*. Maryknoll, New York: Orbis Books, 1989.

Gnanadason, Aruna. *No Longer a Secret: The Church and Violence Against Women*. Geneva: World Council of Churches Publication, 1993.

Goldstein, Rabbi Elyse. *ReVisions*. Toronto: Key Porter Books, 1998.

Haskins, Susan. *Mary Magdalen*. London: HarperCollins,1993.

Hayter, Mary. *The New Eve in Christ*. Grand Rapids: Wm. B. Eerdmans, 1987.

Hebblethwaite, Margaret. *Six New Gospels*. Boston: Cowley Publications, 1994.

Heine, Susanne. *Women and Early Christianity*. Minneapolis: Augsburg Publishing House, 1988.

Maier, Paul L. Trans. and Ed. *Josephus:The Essential Writings*. Grand Rapids: Kregel Publications, 1988.

Kates, Judith A. and Reimer, Gail T. Eds. *Reading Ruth: Contemporary Jewish Women Reclaim a Sacred Story*. New York: Ballantine Books, 1996.

LaCocque, André. *The Feminine Unconventional*. Minneapolis: Fortress Press, 1990.

Laffey, Alice L. *An Introduction to the Old Testament*. Philadelphia: Fortress Press, 1988.

Lohfink, Gerhard. *The Bible: Now I Get It!* Garden City, N.Y.: Doubleday, 1976.

Malone, Mary T. *Women and Christianity. Volume I. The First Thousand Years*. Ottawa: Novalis, 2000.

McFague, Sallie. *Models of God*. Philadelphia: Fortress Press, 1987.

Newsom, C. and S. Ringe, Eds. *The Women's Bible Commentary*. Louisville: Westminster/John Knox, 1992.

Nowak, Gwen. *Miriam of Nazareth: who can find her?* Toronto: Cortleigh House, 2000.

Pagels, Elaine. *Adam, Eve, and the Serpent*. New York: Random House, 1988.

___________. *The Gnostic Gospels*. New York: Random House, 1979.

Peckham, Brian. *History and Prophecy*. New York: Doubleday, 1993.

Phillips, J.A. *Eve: The History of an Idea*. San Francisco: Harper and Row, 1984.

Plaskow, Judith. *Standing Again at Sinai*. New York: HarperCollins, 1990.

Rader, Rosemary. *Breaking Boundaries*. New York: Paulist Press, 1983.

Robins, Wendy S. Ed. *Through the Eyes of a Woman*. Geneva: World Council of Churches Publications, 1995.

Ruether, Rosemary R. Ed. *Religion and Sexism*. New York: Simon and Schuster, 1974.

______. *Mary – the Feminine Face of the Church*. Philadelphia: The Westminster Press, 1977.

Sandars, N. K. Trans. *The Epic of Gilgamesh*. New York: Penguin Books, 1972.

Schaberg, Jane. *The Illegitimacy of Jesus*. New York: Crossroad, 1990.

Spong, John Shelby. *Born of a Woman*. New York: HarperCollins, 1992.

Stegemann E. W. and W. Stegemann. *The Jesus Movement*. Minneapolis: Fortress Press, 1995.

Stanton, Elizabeth Cady. *The Woman's Bible*. Edinburgh: Polygon Books, 1985.

Thurston, Bonnie Bowman. *The Widows*. Minneapolis: Fortress Press, 1989.

Torjesen, Karen Jo. *When Women Were Priests*. New York: HarperCollins, 1993.

Trible, Phyllis. *God and the Rhetoric of Sexuality*. Philadelphia: Fortress Press, 1978.

Weems, Renita. *Just a Sister Away*. San Diego: Lura Media, 1988.

Wilson, Lois Miriam. *Miriam, Mary and Me*. Winfield, B.C.: Wood Lake Books, 1992.

Winter, Miriam Therese. *WomanWisdom*. New York: Crossroad, 1991.

_____. *WomanWitness*. New York: Crossroad, 1992.

_____. *WomanWord*. New York: Crossroad, 1992.

_____. *The Chronicles of Noah and Her Sisters*. New York: Crossroad, 1997.

Young, Serinity, Ed. *An Anthology of Sacred Texts By and About Women*. New York: Crossroad, 1993.

Music Resources

Voices United. The Hymn Book of the United Church of Canada. Etobicoke: The United Church Publishing House, 1996.

Carole A. Etzler: 1180 VT Route 22A, Bridport, VT 05734, U.S.A. CEagle4@aol.com

Carolyn McDade. Living Land, Box 22113, 3806 Albert St., Regina, Sask. S4S 7G7 livingland@cableregina.com

Miriam Therese Winter: Medical Mission Sisters, 77 Sherman St., Hartford, CT 06105, U.S.A.

Resources from Women's Inter-Church Council of Canada. Available in Fall, 2003.

Suite 201 – 394 Bloor St. West, Toronto, ON M5S 1X4 wicc@wicc.org

Hands to End Violence Against Women: Updated and Revised. A study resource with useful tools for groups and congregations who want to address issues of violence against women. Includes workshops, biblical reflection, and liturgical resources.

Anti-Racism Reflection and Action. A tool kit for women's groups and congregations who want to raise awareness about racism and develop strategies to dismantle racism.

About the Author

Bernice Santor received an Honours History degree from McMaster University, a Bachelor of Education certificate from Hamilton Teachers' College and a Master of Theological Studies from Huron University College, The University of Western Ontario in London, Ontario. She was a member of the United Church Women for twenty-five years serving as president in her local congregation as well as on the executive at the presbyterial and conference level. As part of her participation in the Ecumenical Decade of Churches in Solidarity with Women in Church and Society, she attended the closing festival event in Harare, Zimbabwe in 1998. Bernice was a founding member of *Ekklesia*, an ecumenical Christian feminist group of women who meet in London, Ontario. Presently she is a member of the Women's Inter-Church Council of Canada and has served as the chair of the World Day of Prayer committee. Bernice is a quilter, a social activist, a homemaker, a mother and a grandmother. She lives with her husband, Don in Grand Bend, Ontario.